Young people's images of science

Young people's images of science

Rosalind Driver
John Leach
Robin Millar
Phil Scott

Open University Press
Buckingham · Philadelphia

Open University Press
Celtic Court
22 Ballmoor
Buckingham
MK18 1XW

and
1900 Frost Road, Suite 101
Bristol, PA 19007, USA

First Published 1996

A catalogue record of this book is available from the British Library

ISBN 0 335 19381 1 (pb) 0 335 19382 X (hb)

Library of Congress Cataloging-in-Publication Data

Driver, Rosalind.
    Young people's images of science / Rosalind Driver . . . [et al.].
       p. cm.
    Includes bibliographical references and index.
    ISBN 0–335–19381–1 (pbk)   ISBN 0–335–19382–X (hbk)
    1. Science—Study and teaching. 2. Educational psychology.
I. Driver, Rosalind.
Q181.D69   1995
370.15'65—dc20   95–19611
                                                                 CIP

Typeset by Graphicraft Typesetters Limited, Hong Kong
Printed in Great Britain by Biddles Limited, Guildford and Kings Lynn

Contents

List of figures and tables

Preface

This book is the result of a funded research project on which the four of us collaborated. The research project, titled 'The Development of Pupils' Understanding of the Nature of Science', was funded by the Economic and Social Research Council between September 1991 and August 1993. The research project produced a set of eleven working papers under the series title 'Students' Understanding of the Nature of Science'. Details of all aspects of the study, including the complete text of the research instruments and coding schemes used, are presented in these working papers. A complete list of the working papers is given in Appendix 3.

Acknowledgements

The research on which this book is based was supported by a grant from the Economic and Social Research Council of the UK (Grant No. R000233286). Liz Demsetz was involved in the collection and coding of the interview data. We are grateful to her for the care with which this was done. The following people participated in helpful discussions at various stages or commented on drafts of sections of the book: Nancy Brickhouse, Hilary Asoko, Glen Aikenhead and Nick Selley. We would like to acknowledge the contribution that these people have made to our thinking. Finally, we would like to thank Irene Rudling for her patience and care in preparing the manuscript.

Conventions used for presenting extracts from interview transcripts

Extracts from interviews with students are presented at various points in chapters 6, 7 and 9 of this book. For these, we have used the following conventions:

- In all transcripts, the interviewer's comments are indicated by I.
- If only one student is involved in an interchange, the student's comments are indicated by S.
- In extracts taken from interviews with pairs of students, where both students took part in an interchange, the comments of individual students are identified as S1 and S2.
- In extracts taken from interviews involving groups of three of more students (reported in chapter 9), it was not possible to identify reliably, from the audio-taped record, which student was speaking at all times. We have therefore not attempted to indicate individual speakers and simply identify all student comments as S.
- In a passage of interview transcript material, a line space indicates the end of a section of interview. Any subsequent section of transcript is taken either from a different point in the same interview, or from a different interview, with different students.

1 | Introduction

School science and public understanding

There is an important argument that school science, if it is to contribute effectively to improved public understanding of science, must develop students' understanding of the scientific enterprise itself, of the aims and purposes of scientific work, and of the nature of the knowledge it produces. Such an understanding, it is argued, is necessary for students to develop an appreciation of both the power and the limitations of scientific knowledge claims, an appreciation which is necessary for dealing appropriately with the products of science and technology as informed citizens who can participate fully in a modern democracy.

Interest in teaching about the nature of science is apparent in curriculum guidelines in a number of countries. In the UK, the inclusion of an Attainment Target on *The Nature of Science* in the original version of the Science National Curriculum (DES/WO 1989) is a prominent expression of this point of view. The recommendations of the American Association for the Advancement of Science for a curriculum to provide 'Science for All Americans' (AAAS 1989) begin with a chapter entitled 'The Nature of Science', with sub-sections on the scientific world view, scientific enquiry and the scientific enterprise. A series of major international conferences, in 1988, 1991 and 1995, on history and philosophy of science and science teaching, leading to the launch of a new academic journal specializing in this field (*Science and Education*), speak of the current extent of worldwide interest by the science education community in this area.

If the argument that developing learners' understanding of the nature of science is an important aspect of an education in science is accepted, then it would be valuable to know more of learners' ideas about science and scientific knowledge; such knowledge of the baseline from which students begin is important in order to inform curriculum planning and development. Our interest in students' ideas about the nature of science springs primarily from this concern. It has a further root in research on students' ideas about the natural world.

| Students' understanding 'of science'

Over the past twenty-five years, we have learned a great deal about the ideas young people hold about the behaviour of the natural world. Researchers have probed students' understanding of almost every major topic area of science. They have reported in detail on young people's ideas about matter, about the patterns and causes of motion, about photosynthesis in green plants, and many others (see, for example, Driver *et al.* 1994; Pfundt and Duit 1994). This work has revealed many widely shared interpretations and explanations of phenomena and events which differ from the accepted scientific view. So, for instance, we now know that many young people hold the view that plants add to their bulk by taking in extra material ('food') through their roots; the air is seen to play little or no part. Similarly, many see burning as a process in which matter is destroyed; think of constant motion as requiring a force to maintain it; consider that electric current must be used up in lighting a bulb; and so on. Not only are such views widespread, they also prove extremely resistant to change, even through quite carefully constructed teaching programmes.

In probing students' explanations of such natural phenomena, we also catch glimpses of their ideas about what can and cannot be explained, or of what might count as an explanation. We may see whether a student is satisfied with different explanations for different phenomena within a domain, or seeks more general, overarching explanations which apply to a range of situations and examples. We may get insights into where students see explanatory ideas as coming from: whether 'read off' from nature, or imaginatively proposed to account for observed phenomena. And we see the range of ways in which students use observational evidence to check, test and refine explanations. These ideas about science and scientific knowledge are not merely of interest in themselves, they are significant in understanding and interpreting students' ideas about the natural world itself.

So our interest in students' ideas 'about science' has also grown directly out of our involvement in research on young people's understandings of the natural world. Often, it seems as though learners' responses to observations and ideas are constrained and limited in significant ways by their perception of the nature of scientific work and of scientific knowledge itself. The result is that new experiences and information presented in the classroom and laboratory are often interpreted by students in ways that differ from those intended by teachers and curriculum planners. Knowing more about these perceptions may, therefore, help us to understand better the processes of science content learning and hence contribute to more effective teaching.

| Research on students' ideas about science

A study of students' understandings of the nature of science makes science itself the focus of enquiry. Such understandings would include an appreciation of the purposes of science, in seeking explanations of events in the natural world, and of the ways in which science functions as a social institution and interacts with the wider culture, as well as an understanding of the nature and status of scientific knowledge. This is *knowledge about science* as opposed to *scientific knowledge* (knowledge about the natural world). Since one aspect of knowledge about science is 'knowledge about scientific knowledge', it is important to make this distinction as clear as possible. Scientific knowledge is expressed in language which refers to the objects, phenomena and events of the 'real world'. (This is not, of course, to claim that the language simply 'describes' the real world or corresponds to it precisely.) Talk *about scientific knowledge* is different; it is expressed in language which refers to the 'objects' of science itself: theory, observation, law, and so on. When we talk *about scientific knowledge*, we are using a meta-language: a language about a language. Figure 1.1 summarizes these relationships.

Is it reasonable to suppose that school students have ideas about science or, if they do, that these ideas are sufficiently well-founded to merit study? To approach this question, let us first consider the assumptions which underpin research on students' ideas about natural phenomena.

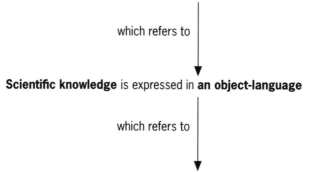

Talk *about* scientific knowledge is expressed in **a meta-language**

which refers to

Scientific knowledge is expressed in **an object-language**

which refers to

The world (reality) is made up of **objects, phenomena, events, etc.**

Figure 1.1 Talk *about* scientific knowledge, scientific knowledge and the world.

Many studies of students' ideas about phenomena in a number of science domains, particularly those which probe ideas prior to formal instruction, are based on the view that we interpret our experiences – both physical and social – by constructing mental models which allow us to explain these experiences and to predict what will happen in new situations. These ideas are then 'tested' in our interactions with the world and in conversation with other people. Those which 'work' well enough for our purposes survive and are consolidated. In this view, the origins of students' untutored views about the world lie in direct experiences of phenomena and in the language we all use to talk about aspects of the world.

Studies of students' understanding *after* an episode of formal instruction have also been undertaken. Underlying many such studies is a view of the learning of accepted bodies of knowledge as an induction into the established view; the learner's task is not so much to 'construct' or 'discover' a point of view, as to make an already existing view their own. This, however, is not seen as a simple matter of 'transfer' from teacher to taught. Instead, it is recognized that learners frequently interpret taught ideas and models in a manner which diverges from that which the teacher intends. Again this perspective on learning makes it interesting and important to discover how students are thinking about phenomena in the domain in question, as a means of monitoring the effectiveness of a teaching intervention.

A study of students' ideas about the nature of science is based on similar assumptions: that students' have ideas about scientific work and scientific knowledge prior to any formal science instruction, and that the views they hold after such instruction may differ from those which we would believe to be explicit or, more likely, implicit in that instruction. Their ideas may not, of course, be expressed in the usual meta-language of science. But students, even at primary school stage, are likely to have ideas about scientists and scientific work. These may come from their exposure to images of science and scientists in the wider culture, particularly in films, television programmes (including cartoons) and comics, and, increasingly as they get older, from the messages – both implicit and explicit – in school science. We might say that they have developed a mental 'representation' of various aspects of the scientific endeavour.

Everyday experience also tells us that students are likely to be able, from an early age, to offer an account of *why* they consider a fact, or an explanation, about the natural world to be true or false. In other words, students have elements, at least, of a developing epistemology. *Epistemology* is the branch of philosophy which deals with theories of knowledge. It seeks to probe the distinctions between *believing* something to be the case, and *knowing* that it is; it is concerned with questions of our grounds for knowledge, and of the relationship between methods of enquiry and the knowledge they produce. Of course, students' epistemologies may not be consistent, or expressed in the terms a philosopher would use. That is not the issue. What we are claiming is that there are good grounds for supposing that students *can* entertain epistemological questions and can express their reasoning in words, however informally. Such questions *can* make sense from a student's perspective.

A study of students' understanding of the nature of science

This book is, essentially, an account of a research project, undertaken to elicit and to describe the range and nature of school students' understandings of the nature of science. We have outlined very briefly some of the reasons why we came to regard a study of students' knowledge about science as interesting and potentially valuable to the enterprise of understanding and perhaps improving science education. As we have argued in the previous section, we embarked on the study with the working assumption that school students, from an early age, are likely to have constructed mental representations of various aspects of the scientific enterprise, and to have developed functional epistemologies about natural phenomena and events. For reasons which we will discuss more fully later, the features of students' representations of the nature of science which we decided to focus on were their views on *the purposes of scientific work*, their understanding of *the nature and status of scientific knowledge* (including the relation between evidence and explanation, the role of experimentation and the nature of theory) and their understanding of *science as a social enterprise.*

When we began to plan the study in 1991, the current version of the Science National Curriculum for England and Wales contained an explicit strand on *The Nature of Science*. We chose, therefore, to focus our attention on students in the age range covered by National Curriculum provisions. We decided, for reasons which are discussed more fully in Chapter 5, to design a cross-age study, giving the same task to samples of students of three different ages: 9, 12 and 16 years. For most tasks, we chose to interview pairs of students at each age, rather than collecting answers to written questions, or observing ordinary classroom activities. The approach we adopted, and the probes we developed and used, are described and explained in detail in Chapter 5.

Our raw data, then, came in the form of interviews, usually with pairs of students. These were tape-recorded and later transcribed. Each was then read and the separate sections classified into categories which characterized the range of students' responses. We tried, so far as possible, not to pre-judge what these categories should be, but to develop them from the data. By using the same tasks with students of each age, we were then able to look for differences between 9-, 12- and 16-year-olds' responses, and so to begin to paint a picture of the ways in which understandings seem to change with age and experience. Again we will describe and illustrate this approach to the analysis of our data in more detail later and will present and discuss the patterns of response which we found most interesting.

| The structure of the book

This chapter has tried to provide a preliminary overview of some of the main themes of the book. Some key terms have been explained and some of our underlying assumptions declared. In Chapter 2, we will look in more detail at the arguments for giving the nature of science a more prominent place in the school science curriculum, setting out more fully the reasons why this aspect of science education is currently a focus of worldwide attention and interest. In Chapter 3, we review the major strands in thinking about the nature of science. The chapter is an overview, following a broadly chronological sequence, of the major schools of thought about science and scientific knowledge, and our grounds for confidence in it. It enables us to identify, among the competing positions, a core of key ideas and issues about the nature of science which might form the basis for an empirical study. Chapter 4 then looks at previous research on students' ideas about the nature of science. It does not aim to be an exhaustive review, but focuses instead on the studies which have most influenced our own thinking as we designed this study. It also helps us to specify more clearly the aspects of the nature of science we want to explore. This process is completed in Chapter 5, which draws the first half of the book together. This describes in detail, and justifies, the particular approach we chose to adopt, the research questions we chose to focus upon, and the research methods and tools we developed and used to explore students' ideas.

Chapters 6–9 then present and discuss the main findings of the study. Chapter 6 looks at students' ideas about the boundary between science and non-science, by asking which of a set of questions would be of interest to scientists and which would not. Chapter 7, which is the longest by far of the chapters reporting the data, explores the issues which lie at the heart of the study, concerning students' ideas about the nature of scientific knowledge and the methods of scientific enquiry, and their relationship. Data from four quite different interview probes are presented and discussed, and a three-level classification of students' epistemological reasoning is gradually drawn out. The lowest level of this classification is reasoning grounded in *phenomena*; the highest level is reasoning which uses imagined *models*. Between these, we identify a frequently used middle level – a form of reasoning based on *relationships* between quantities (or variables). This emergent classification is then set out explicitly and its implications explored in Chapter 8. The last of the data chapters, Chapter 9, looks at students' understanding of science as a social enterprise. It explores students' ideas about the internal social structure of the scientific community, about the relationship between science and the wider society, and about the influence (if any) of these social linkages on scientific knowledge and practices. We did not succeed in devising tasks which enabled 9- or 12-year-olds to engage with these issues, so this part of the study is based on 16-year-olds only. The chapter reports on a classroom-based task designed to probe ideas about the causes of disagreements about scientific knowledge, and the means by which these might be resolved.

Finally, in Chapter 10, we summarize the main findings of the study and draw out some possible implications for the school science curriculum, focusing in particular on its role in promoting better public understanding of science.

2 | Why does understanding of the nature of science matter?

The aims of science education

We have argued in Chapter 1 that it is reasonable to suppose that young people have ideas about the work that scientists do and about the scientific enterprise in general, and that they can entertain questions about the grounds for holding particular views about the behaviour of the natural world. These ideas come from exposure to media images of science and scientists, from everyday experience of the technological products of scientific knowledge and from the kinds of explanations which are used in everyday talk. School science, however it is structured and presented, provides further implicit (and perhaps also explicit) ideas about scientific work and scientific knowledge. The current high level of interest among science educators in teaching about the nature of science, to which we referred briefly in Chapter 1, reflects the view that this aspect of science is important and should be treated explicitly. But *why* do we consider it important that school students learn something of the nature of science? This question is important, because only when we have answered it does it make sense to go on to ask: *what* would we wish them to know about the nature of science? That question in turn matters because our answer to it identifies the ideas we would wish to probe in a study of students' ideas.

Any answer to the question 'why should students learn about the nature of science?' depends, of course, on the answer to a prior question: 'why should students learn science?' It is a striking feature of education systems the world over that science is invariably accorded high status, and allocated considerable resources, throughout the years of compulsory schooling. In low-income countries, where difficult choices about resourcing are inevitable, science is a priority subject. In technologically advanced countries, science provision for all students throughout their school career is becoming the norm. The status of science as a 'core subject' in the National Curriculum for England and Wales, to be studied by all young people throughout the years of compulsory schooling from age 5 to age 16 (DES/WO 1989), is just one example. One important reason for this emphasis on science is the perceived need to maintain a pool of qualified people from whom the scientists, technologists and technicians of the future may be drawn.

In any education system, however, most of those who study science at school will not go on to use their science understanding directly in their future careers. If science is a core subject for all pupils, the proportion who will use science for career purposes is likely to be relatively small. For the majority, science is part of their general education – one aspect of their preparation for life. The aim here is to improve *scientific literacy*; that is, increase the numbers of 'scientifically literate' adults in society and hence to improve *public understanding of science*. In practice, of course, the same science curriculum has to do both these jobs: of providing the first stages of a training in science for a minority of students, and giving access to basic scientific literacy for the majority. These two purposes can often appear in tension, and they may well lead to differences in curriculum content and emphasis. But they share two common aims. First, both have the aim of helping students come to an understanding of some parts of the corpus of substantive scientific knowledge. The priorities and the depth of treatment may differ, but in so far as an understanding of the nature of science and scientific knowledge underpins successful science learning, this would apply equally to both. Second, scientists are also citizens. The goal of a broad scientific literacy applies as much to the aspiring specialist as to the student who will choose a non-science career path. Scientific expertise is limited to a narrow area of specialism; both as an individual and as a citizen, a scientist may have to take decisions which involve ideas outside his or her narrow area of expertise. In such areas, the scientist is, in many respects, an educated 'lay person'. And scientists, *qua* scientist, need to be able to communicate their specialist knowledge to non-expert audiences, sensitive to the possibilities of misunderstanding about the nature of scientific knowledge. We would also wish them to be aware of broader issues concerning their responsibilities for the directions and emphases in their work, and to be mindful of the dependence of the scientific enterprise on wider societal support, both tangible and intangible. For these reasons, it is important that scientists develop sophisticated understandings of the institutional nature of science and its social and political control (Husén *et al.* 1992).

In this chapter, we will therefore be considering the question 'why does understanding of the nature of science matter?' from the perspective of a science curriculum which aims to provide access to basic scientific literacy for all students and hence to improve public understanding of science. We address the question in two main stages. First, we review the arguments in the literature for improving scientific literacy and consider what aspects of science may be important curriculum goals in order to achieve this. We then consider how an understanding of the nature of science – that is, an understanding *about* science – relates to such curriculum goals and hence to promoting public understanding of science. The core of the argument which we will be developing is that an understanding of the nature of science is an essential aspect of public understanding of science.

| Scientific literacy as a curriculum aim

Arguments for teaching science to all in order to improve public under-standing of science come from scientists, educationalists and government alike. Indeed, it has become almost commonplace to argue that: 'The impact of scientific and technological developments on our everyday lives is so great that no one can afford to be ignorant of these developments' (Giere 1991: 1).

In Britain and the United States, two powerful and prestigious scientists' organizations, the Royal Society and the American Association for the Advancement of Science (AAAS), have recently published reports express-ing concern about the level of understanding of science among the wider public (Royal Society 1985a, 1985b; AAAS 1989). The authors of the Royal Society report propose that:

> Everybody needs some understanding of science, its accomplishments and its limitations, whether or not they are themselves scientists or engineers. Improving that understanding is not a luxury: it is a vital investment in the future well-being of our society.
>
> (Royal Society 1985b: 1)

The AAAS authors adopt a more urgent tone:

> The life-enhancing potential of science and technology cannot be realized unless the public in general comes to understand science, mathematics and technology and to acquire scientific habits of mind; without a scientifically literate population, the outlook for a better world is not promising.
>
> (AAAS 1989: 13)

Both reports argue that science education is essential for all students if they are to participate fully in a society that places increasing reliance on science and technology. Some understanding of science is necessary, they argue, if the wider public is to be able to exercise appropriate democratic control over the purposes and directions of scientific and technological advance. This in turn may lead to a stronger sense of ownership of the sci-entific enterprise and to greater public support for science and technology.

Some commentators have focused on what scientific literacy is thought to be *for*. Shen (1975) writes of three 'functional scientific literacies': practical scientific literacy enables an individual to cope with basic everyday problems; civic scientific literacy enables citizens to contribute to discussions about science-related issues as they manifest themselves in particular social contexts; and cultural scientific literacy enables citizens to appreciate science as a major cultural achievement. Layton *et al.* (1993) even question the utility of a general notion of 'scientific literacy' by extending Shen's idea to include other functional scientific literacies, such as industrial scientific literacy (of management and workers in specific occupational contexts) and recreational scientific literacy (related to specific hobbies or pastimes). Others have taken a functional approach, while retaining a unitary notion of scientific literacy; Giere (1991) and Hann *et al.* (1992), for instance, focus on the ability to evaluate media reports on scientific matters.

The cultural importance of science – Shen's third functional literacy – also informs the AAAS (1989) curriculum proposal, which contains a section on 'historical perspectives'. 'Some episodes in the history of the scientific endeavour', it is argued, 'are of surpassing significance to our cultural heritage' (AAAS 1989: 111). Arguments, and specimen materials, for including history of science within the school science curriculum have a long history (see, for example, Klopfer 1964; Russell 1981; Matthews 1994). The inclusion in the first version of the National Curriculum for England and Wales (DES/WO 1989) of an Attainment Target called *The Nature of Science*, which drew heavily on historical contexts and examples, and the retention of this element in later revisions (DES/WO 1991; DFE/WO 1995), albeit in a less prominent role, is a recent example.

Thomas and Durant (1987) provide an overview of arguments in the literature for promoting public understanding of science, arguments which have much in common with Shen's functional scientific literacies. The most important of these are:

- The *economic* argument: we need a supply of qualified scientists to maintain and develop the industrial processes on which national prosperity depends.
- The *utilitarian* argument: everyone needs to understand some science to manage the technological objects and processes they encounter in everyday life.
- The *democratic* argument: in a democracy, it is desirable that as many people as possible can participate in decision-making; many important issues involve science and technology; everyone should understand science in order to be able to participate in discussion, debate and decision-making about these.
- The *cultural* argument: science is a major cultural achievement; everyone should be enabled to appreciate it.
- The *moral* argument: that the practice of science embodies norms and commitments, which are of wider value.

The first of these relates most obviously to the vocational purposes of science education, in preparing the qualified scientists and technologists of the future. It is also argued, however, that a scientifically literate population is more likely to have a positive attitude towards science and technology and hence to be generally more supportive of scientific and technological developments (OST 1993). The other four arguments relate to the wider purposes of science education as part of the general education of all students.

While improving 'scientific literacy' and hence 'public understanding of science' are widely advocated as educational goals, there is less agreement about what, precisely, a person would need to know, understand or be able to do, to be regarded as 'scientifically literate', or about precisely what aspects of science we might wish the public to 'understand'. The Royal Society (1985b: 2) proposes that: 'Understanding includes not just the facts of science, but also the method and its limitations as well as an appreciation of the practical and social implications'.

In *Science for all Americans*, the AAAS (1989) proposes a learning programme which encompasses a formidable range of content, spanning the physical and life sciences, technology, engineering and mathematics. The programme also includes an understanding of the nature of science, of mathematics and of technology, and the development of scientific 'habits of mind'.

All those who have written about public understanding of science agree that it involves at least three aspects:

1 An understanding of some aspects of *science content*. That is, it involves an understanding of some of the facts, laws, concepts and theories which make up the corpus of consensually accepted scientific knowledge about the natural world. There can, of course, still be much dispute about which items of content are necessary, or have priority.

2 An understanding of the *scientific approach to enquiry*. As a second aspect of science understanding, Miller (1983) identifies 'understanding the scientific approach'. This he sees, for example, as involving the ability to define 'scientific study' and to identify differences between the sciences and non-sciences or pseudo-sciences, such as astrology. Wynne (1990: 28), on the other hand, writes of 'understanding about its [science's] methods (so as to appreciate its limits as well as its powers)'. A recent major survey of the understanding of science of the British public (Durant *et al.* 1989: 12) sought to measure 'understanding of the processes of scientific enquiry' as well as scientific knowledge. It is important, in our view, to recognize that this aspect of public understanding of science involves not only an understanding of empirical enquiry procedures, but also of the role of theoretical and conceptual ideas in framing any empirical enquiry and in interpreting its outcomes.

3 An understanding of *science as a social enterprise*. Wynne (1990) argues that the public encounters science through its institutional representatives and responds to it, not as 'pure knowledge' but in terms of the human and institutional face it presents; and that a key element of public understanding of science is an 'understanding about its forms of institutional embedding and control' (p. 28). Wynne suggests that many members of the public 'understand' this rather well. His argument for a stronger focus on this aspect of public understanding is, however, directed at science policy-makers rather than educators. From a more explicitly educational perspective, Miller (1983: 40) identifies, as a third strand of scientific literacy, 'understanding of science policy issues'. This, though important, seems unnecessarily narrow. A term which has become widely used by curriculum developments emphasizing this third aspect of science understanding is 'Science–Technology–Society' (STS) (Cheek 1992; Solomon 1993; Solomon and Aikenhead 1994). This makes clear the focus on the interrelationships between these three elements. It includes an understanding both of the relations between science and the wider society and of science as a social institution (Ziman 1967, 1978). It might be put more briefly as an understanding of 'science-in-society' and of 'science-as-society'.

Understanding the nature of science: an essential component of scientific literacy

In the previous section, we described three aspects of science which it is widely agreed are necessary for a public understanding of science:

- understanding some aspects of science content;
- understanding the scientific approach to enquiry;
- understanding science as a social enterprise.

In this section, we consider the extent to which 'an understanding of the nature of science' itself is integral to each of these aspects. First, perhaps, we need to make clear what we mean by 'an understanding of the nature of science'. In the broadest terms, we mean those ideas which a student (or an adult) has *about science*, as distinct from their ideas about the natural world itself (their 'scientific knowledge'). At the heart of this is their understanding of the nature and status of scientific knowledge: how the body of public knowledge called science has been established and is added to; what our grounds are for considering it reliable knowledge; how the agreement which characterizes much of science (and essentially of all school science) is maintained. This in turn involves an understanding of the social organization and practices of science, whereby knowledge claims are 'transmuted' into public knowledge, and of the influence of science or the wider culture, and vice versa. Issues surrounding the application of scientific knowledge in practical situations are an important focus, as the lack of consensus about these invites a re-evaluation of claims about the status of particular kinds of knowledge. A related issue is about the purpose of scientific work (in seeking explanation) and the boundaries of its areas of interest.

How does such 'an understanding of the nature of science' relate to each of the three aspects of public understanding of science identified above? The relationship is clearest and easiest to articulate for the second and third aspects, so we will start with a consideration of these.

An understanding of the scientific approach to enquiry, as we have already pointed out, involves an epistemological dimension: all empirical enquiry is planned and carried out within a framework imposed by the conceptual and theoretical structures which the enquirer brings to bear on it. Indeed, the failure to recognize and incorporate this epistemological dimension is a major weakness of many curriculum treatments of scientific enquiry (see, for example, NCC 1991) and of arguments for an investigative component in the curriculum (see, for example, Coles and Gott 1993). Similarly, epistemological considerations underpin an understanding of the limits of application of the scientific approach and of the demarcation between sciences and non-sciences. Some explicit reflection on the nature of scientific knowledge, the role of observation and experiment, the nature of theory, and the relationship between evidence and theory, is an essential component of this aspect of understanding of science.

The third aspect, an understanding of *science as a social enterprise*, is entirely concerned with the knowledge *about science*, rather than knowledge about the natural world itself (scientific knowledge). An explicit understanding of the social organization of science, of its mechanisms for receiving, checking and validating knowledge claims, and an awareness of the possible influence of social commitments and values on the choices and interpretations that scientists make, and of the influence on the wider culture of scientific ideas and artefacts, are part of what we mean by 'an understanding of the nature of science'.

If we turn now to the first aspect, an understanding of some science content, the relationship to an understanding of the nature of science is perhaps less immediately clear. Scientific knowledge – knowledge of the natural world – is not, however, read directly off 'the book of nature'. Learning science content involves coming to accept a set of categories (objects and properties) as providing useful and natural ways of viewing events. These are what philosophers would term 'metaphysical commitments' (Harré 1972). So, for example, when we learn Newton's Laws of Motion, we accept the idea of 'force' – as it is defined within the Newtonian view – and of 'mass' and 'acceleration' as useful categories through which to interpret examples of motion. In learning any scientific explanation, we also have to learn about its areas of applicability, the limits to its usefulness. One important element of this is appreciating that science proceeds by separating out single features of complex situations, and isolating the thing we are interested in from the masking effects of other variables, to build up understanding. So science invokes idealizations like point masses, frictionless surfaces and ideal gases. This, of course, means that there is always an issue about the applicability of this understanding to contexts which are more complex, where real objects are involved and different factors interact. So an understanding of science content knowledge implies an understanding of the nature of that knowledge.

From an educational perspective, it is also important in this context to recognize that our aim is not that our students should be able simply to recall scientific facts, laws and theories. Most teachers would agree that we want them to know *why* scientific ideas and theories are reasonable, rather than simply to assent to them. Munby (1982), for example, argues strongly for science teaching which promotes 'intellectual independence' and aims to provide students with 'all the resources necessary for judging the truth of knowledge independently of other people' (p. 31). This draws upon the philosophical distinction between 'knowledge' and 'belief'. To 'know' something, a person must not simply believe it to be the case, but be able to provide grounds (usually in the form of evidence) for their belief. Norris (1992) qualifies Munby's argument by pointing out that we do want students to understand scientific ideas for which we cannot provide direct first-hand evidence. He argues that the aim should be to provide a basis for 'rational trust ... based on two elements (a) a recognition of expertise (Siegel 1988); and (b) knowledge of the general shape that a justification would have to take, of the general sorts of considerations that scientists count as justification' (p. 216).

Siegel (1988), cited by Norris, discusses the factors that enable the recognition of expertise. This is also explored by Funtowicz and Ravetz (1987), who provide a set of criteria based on this and other factors (such as peer acceptance and colleague consensus) for evaluating the 'pedigree' of a scientific knowledge claim. These issues are of real practical significance for individuals deciding whether to accept expert advice (for example, from a doctor) or how to respond to a local or national issue which concerns them. For all these reasons, then, an understanding of science content requires an understanding of the nature of science.

Why does understanding of the nature of science matter? Arguments in the literature

In the previous section, we argued that an understanding of the nature of science is an essential, indeed an integral, component of public understanding of science. We now return to the most important arguments in the literature for promoting the public understanding of science, which were presented at the beginning of the chapter, and examine the extent to which an explicit understanding of the nature of science is a necessary requirement in each case.

A *utilitarian* argument | an understanding of the nature of science is necessary if people are to make sense of the science and manage the technological objects and processes they encounter in everyday life

Some practical decisions and choices involve scientific knowledge. In making such decisions, however, people must first decide whether a piece of knowledge is applicable to the case in hand. Then they must form a judgement about the reliability and the possible limitations of the knowledge they possess. These involve *epistemological* issues. Decisions about whether to place trust in an 'expert', such as a doctor, are also often involved. This brings in a *sociological* dimension of understanding, in assessing the credentials of the knowledge provider as well as of the knowledge provided. Making practical use of scientific knowledge therefore involves an understanding of the grounds for confidence in the knowledge involved and in the sources of that knowledge; in other words, an understanding of the nature of scientific knowledge.

It is also implicit in much informal science education (in newspaper features, television programmes, and so on) that people would feel more 'at home' with the products of science if they had a better understanding of the ideas involved. This would include not only the material products of science (tools, appliances, materials, and so on), but also its intellectual products (the conceptual tools which science provides). A key element in such understanding is the ability to assimilate information about scientific matters from a variety of informal information sources. Giere (1991) developed a learning programme to help first- and second-year college students 'acquire cognitive skills in *understanding* and *evaluating* scientific material as found in college textbooks and in a wide variety of both popular and professional printed sources' (p. iii). He argued that:

> Assimilating scientific information requires some conception of what science is all about and some special skills in evaluating the information one receives. Here, then, is a general reason why anyone should develop some understanding of scientific reasoning. This skill is necessary if you are to take full advantage of the scientific information that is increasingly important for functioning effectively in both your professional and your personal life.
>
> (Giere 1991: 2)

His programme for teaching the 'skill' of scientific reasoning centres on developing an understanding of the nature of scientific knowledge, using the model shown in Fig. 2.1. Giere argues that understanding media reports of science depends on realizing that theoretical knowledge in science takes the form of a conjectural model, predictions from which are compared with observation. Underpinning this is an understanding of the purpose of science, as providing explanations for phenomena, and of the distinction between science and technology.

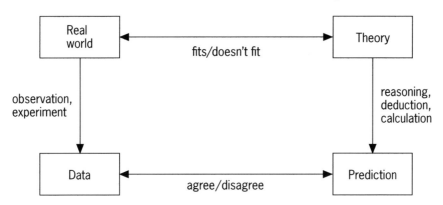

Figure 2.1   A model of scientific reasoning (after Giere 1991).

Another, quite distinct argument that an understanding of the nature of science is useful underpins the so-called 'process approach' to science. This identifies 'the nature of science' with a method of enquiry, through claims, for example, that 'the essential characteristic of education in science is that it introduces pupils to the methods of science' (DES/WO 1985:3). In this view, science is portrayed as a powerful, and quite general, method of enquiry which can be learnt and then used in a wide range of other contexts, both scientific and non-scientific. This method is then analysed into a set of 'processes' such as observing, classifying, predicting, hypothesizing, inferring, and so on. Curriculum packages which have articulated this approach include *Science – A Process Approach* (AAAS 1967), *Warwick Process Science* (Screen 1986), *Science in Process* (ILEA 1988) and *Techniques for the Assessment of Practical Skills in Foundation Science (TAPS 1)* (Bryce *et al.* 1983). In such schemes, students follow activities intended to develop, or to assess, their 'process skills'; the process terminology of observation, inference, prediction, hypothesis, and so on is explicitly taught, on the grounds that, by reflecting on the cognitive 'processes' they are using, students will be able to learn these and transfer them to new situations. They will thus come to appreciate the power and utility of the scientific method of enquiry.

This approach has been criticized as presenting an unhelpful and misleading image of scientific enquiry (Finlay 1983; Millar and Driver 1987; Wellington 1989; Hodson 1991). The 'processes of science' also encompass those processes by which scientific knowledge claims are developed, tested and incorporated into consensual public knowledge. There is also little empirical evidence to support the idea of transferable general 'process skills'. The process approach also tends to portray science simply as empirical enquiry. But, as we have argued in this chapter, scientific enquiry depends on a conceptual framework to guide empirical investigation; conversely, understanding of science content depends on an understanding of the nature of that knowledge. The methods used in scientific enquiry are intimately bound up with the conceptual structures of science, each depending upon the other. Public understanding of science depends, in our view, on a more sophisticated appreciation of this interrelationship than is implicit in the process approach.

| A *democratic* argument | an understanding of the nature of science is necessary if people are to make sense of socioscientific issues and participate in the decision-making process |

Many policy decisions have a science dimension. Decisions are made at various levels – from local to national – about waste disposal, energy policy, genetic engineering, emissions of carbon dioxide, and so on. We will refer to such issues, which are of broad social interest and involve a science dimension, as *socioscientific* issues. The democratic argument for promoting public understanding of science focuses on the understandings needed to participate in the debates surrounding such issues and in the decision-making process itself.

Clearly, some science content knowledge is necessary to understand particular socioscientific issues. But much more than this is involved in any dispute. Often there is consensus about the basic science relating to the issue, but there is dispute about how the laboratory findings relate to the complex and messy real-world situation. Disagreement is not about fundamental theoretical models but about how (or indeed if) they apply. This may be tied up with uncertainties about the reliability of some of the data available, or about the relevance of such data in a new context, or about models of the complex interactions involved. In a few cases, the dispute may extend as far as questioning the basic scientific understandings involved; if so, an understanding that scientific explanation is based on models which are tentative and conjectural becomes important.

In other words, an understanding of the issues requires not just knowledge of science content, but also an understanding of the nature of science and scientific knowledge. How, Collins and Shapin (1986) ask, can the public interpret disagreements between scientific experts if scientific knowledge is seen as secure and reliable information, 'read off from the book of nature'? They conclude that 'scientists, it will be thought, are all incompetents, or liars, or intellectuals available for hire to powerful interest groups' (p. 76), and that this will 'generate profound disillusionment about what is taken to be science as a whole' (p. 75). Their plea is for a stronger focus in the curriculum on science-in-the-making (Shapin 1992; Collins and Pinch 1993), showing more clearly the social processes by which knowledge is negotiated and agreed and emphasizing science as 'expertise about the natural world', rather than 'certain' knowledge.

Socioscientific issues attract media attention and many media reports deal with them. The ability to assimilate information from published sources, discussed above in relation to the utilitarian argument, is, perhaps, of even greater relevance here. Millar and Wynne (1988) provide direct evidence of the conflicts which can arise when a simplistic understanding of scientific knowledge is brought to bear on media reports of a complex socioscientific issue. So, for example, in the aftermath of Chernobyl, people wanted unequivocal statements about the safety or otherwise of specific local practices (such as eating certain vegetables), while scientists provided qualified and abstract general information about radiation levels. Millar and Wynne argue that assimilating information from UK newspaper reports after the Chernobyl disaster depended upon a quite sophisticated understanding of the processes of generation and validation of scientific knowledge, and an awareness of the inherent uncertainty of the data available and the knowledge claims made.

A *cultural* argument	an understanding of the nature of science is necessary in order to appreciate science as a major element of contemporary culture

Scientific knowledge is a major – indeed, many would say, *the* major – achievement of our culture. A cultural approach to science education would seek to communicate an appreciation of the elegant and powerful structures of ideas we have developed for understanding natural phenomena and events. It would emphasize the major landmarks in our understanding of the natural world, and the major figures and events in the history of science. This would inevitably require an understanding of epistemological issues and ideas, and would raise questions, of a sociological kind, about the relationship of ideas and their origins to the social context within which they emerge.

An understanding of contemporary science is also important. This would involve knowing about the institutional framework and processes of science, its organization into disciplines, sub-disciplines, research groups and so on, its methods of funding, its systems of recognition and reward. One compelling reason why these ideas matter is because science demands considerable resources from the wider society, justifying these demands on grounds which range from the utilitarian (in the case of much medical research) to the cultural (in the cases of astronomy and high-energy particle physics). Public funding on the scale involved requires that the public understand and, in the main, share the aims and aspirations of the scientific enterprise and understand how resources are used on society's behalf.

A *moral* argument	learning about the nature of science can help develop awareness of the nature of science, and in particular the norms of the scientific community, embodying moral commitments which are of general value

This argument draws on views such as those of Merton (1942), who identified four institutional norms of science (universalism, communism, disinterestedness and organized scepticism); these he saw as providing 'moral as well as technical prescriptions' (p. 68). Although individual scientists may deviate from these norms, they describe values to which the community as a whole subscribes. Bronowski (1964) notes with approval the way in which the society of science maintains its stability, while permitting – even encouraging – criticism of ideas and freedom of thought. Rapoport (1957) writes of a 'scientific approach to ethics'. He argues that certain ethical principles are inherent in scientific practice:

> the conviction that there exists objective truth; that there exist rules of evidence for discovering it; that, on the basis of this objective truth, unanimity is possible and desirable; and that unanimity must be achieved by independent arrivals at convictions – that is, by examination of evidence, not through coercion, personal argument, or appeal to authority.
>
> (Rapoport 1957: 796)

More recently, and from a quite different epistemological position, Harré (1986: 1) has written that:

> the scientific community exhibits a model or ideal of rational co-operation set within a strict moral order, the whole having no parallel in any other human activity. And this despite the all-too-human characteristics of the actual members of that community seen as just another social order.

Such views, however, are often dismissed as scientism, the inappropriate use of ideas drawn from science in pursuit of non-scientific goals and purposes (see, for example, Cameron and Edge 1979). There is little evidence that scientists adhere to these norms, to a greater extent than any other comparable social group, in contexts outside science, and the extent to which they are honoured within science has also been questioned (Barnes and Dolby 1970).

A *science* *learning* argument	an understanding of the nature of science supports successful learning of science content

The final argument we want to consider concerns the role of an understanding of the nature of science in facilitating the learning of science itself; that is, in coming to an understanding of ideas about the behaviour of the natural world. Students in science classes are exposed to a range of experiences, including direct observation of phenomena, discussion of those observations with classmates and with the teacher, and explanation and exposition of ideas by the teacher. Their grasp of the purposes of these experiences is, however, usually part of the taken-for-granted context of science lessons. Many students, however, may not appreciate that the aim of science is to establish explanations for the behaviour of natural objects and phenomena which can command widespread acceptance. Some may simply see science as the accummulation, by observation and measurement, of 'facts' about the natural world. Others may confuse science with technology, and see the aim as the development of new and better artefacts and materials.

Also, unless care is taken, many students may come to think that scientific ideas, laws and theories 'emerge' from observational data. If they do not appreciate that scientific laws and theories are conjectural and cannot see where an explanation comes from, they may either adopt a passive (rote) learning style which is inefficient at best, or decide that science is not for them. Consider, for example, a student in a class which has carried out some simple observations on the effects produced when plastic rods are rubbed with a cloth and then held near some light objects. In discussion, the teacher labels this effect 'charging' and may then move on to an explanation based on the idea of transfer of electrons by rubbing. Unless care is taken to stress that this is offered as a *possible* explanation (which, although it commands wide acceptance, could not be said to 'follow' from what has been observed), some students may misunderstand the nature of the argument. If this sort of experience is repeated, students may become demotivated, believing that they cannot see the connections that are obvious to others, and become 'turned off' science. So it is important that scientific generalizations and theoretical explanations are presented to children as conjectures (or hypotheses, hunches, guesses), which can be checked out against the data – and not as 'deductions' from what has been observed.

There is some evidence to suggest that such metacognitive knowledge can support conceptual understanding in science. Shapiro (1989, 1994) looks in detail at six children's ideas about themselves as learners of science and about the status of scientific knowledge. She shows that for these students, progress in learning ideas about light was closely related to their view of science and of how to best learn science. Those who valued the scientific perspective and saw science learning as something to which they could contribute were more successful at learning science content. Shapiro suggests a model of the science curriculum in which pupil and teacher become 'co-architects of learning', both sharing ideas about phenomena and viewing science as one (important) perspective. Songer and Linn (1991) also investigated the relationship between student epistemologies of science and conceptual learning. They report that students who view science knowledge as revisable (dynamic) rather than fixed (static) were less likely to believe that learning science depended on memorization and achieved a more integrated understanding of the topic of study (in the case of their research, elementary thermodynamics).

Understanding the relationship between evidence and explanation has been seen by several researchers as critical to science learning, since making sense of scientific explanations often requires learners to consider a theory in relation to the evidence presented to them. Kuhn *et al.* (1988) investigated students' abilities to use evidence appropriately in testing theoretical explanations. They found that younger students appear to have difficulty distinguishing between evidence and theory and that students' commitment to a theory influenced their interpretation of evidence. Carey and her co-workers (1989) argue that children need to understand that, in science, observations are made purposefully, and comment that:

> Students are not challenged to utilise . . . process skills in exploring, developing and evaluating their own ideas about natural phenomena. Rather, instruction in the skills and methods of science is conceived as being outside the context of genuine inquiry. Thus, there is no context for addressing the nature and purpose of scientific inquiry, or the nature of scientific knowledge.
>
> (Carey *et al.* 1989: 514–15)

Carey *et al.* report that students can be taught these ideas about science through instruction designed for that purpose. This approach requires students not only to 'do' laboratory work, but also to think about how their investigations relate to the ideas they are developing. Reflection on laboratory work has also been proposed by others (Driver and Oldham 1986; Millar 1987; Gunstone and Champagne 1990; Solomon 1991) as important in helping students' learning of science content. It is argued, for example, that students benefit from considering the range of ideas that their classmates may have to describe the same phenomenon and developing ways of evaluating these explanations. Through such interactions, students can come to appreciate the criteria on which judgements in science are made.

More generally, Hodson (1988) has argued that, since learning science involves reconstructions of meaning analogous to 'scientific revolutions' (in the sense of T.S. Kuhn 1962), learners would be assisted by having attention drawn to the similarities between their own learning and the historical progress in scientific understanding. Solomon (1991) justifies the inclusion of the history of science in a similar way by suggesting that having students reflect on events in the history of science will help them to construct better understandings of the ways in which their own learning develops. Duschl (1990) focuses on the central role of theory in scientific explanations. He argues that, unless learners know how scientific theories are developed and evaluated, progress in science will appear as a series of inexplicable changes. As a curricular goal, knowledge of how theories are generated in scientific communities is, he suggests, at least as important as understanding the theories themselves; these ideas help students to understand better their own learning in science, a point which echoes the findings of Shapiro and Linn and Songer discussed above. Furthermore, Duschl proposes that students need to appreciate that there are different kinds of theories (core theories, frontier theories) and that the criteria which scientific communities use to categorize theories in this way, so that they are better able to distinguish between legitimate and 'crank' theories.

As a final comment to this section, it may be worth considering the possible link between making the nature of scientific knowledge more transparent to students and maintaining their continuing interest in scientific studies. In other words, there may be a link between the science learning argument and the economic argument for public understanding of science.

| Review and summary

In this chapter, we have set out a range of arguments which can be found in the literature for introducing students to ideas about the nature of science. In the process, some answers have also emerged to the question: what would we wish students to understand about the nature of science? At the heart of many of the arguments is the claim that students need to have some explicit understanding of the nature of scientific knowledge, appreciating the conjectural and hypothetical nature of laws and theories and the possible limits of applicability of ideas developed in laboratory contexts to more complex and messy real-world situations. Implicit in this is an understanding of the aim of the scientific endeavour, in seeking to understand the natural world (and distinguishing this, for example, from the rather different purposes of technology). In several arguments, an understanding of the social structure of the scientific community and an appreciation of the mutual influence of scientific ideas and ideas from the wider culture are important, in the contexts of democratic accountability and of appreciating the major role which science plays and has played in shaping our culture.

The three features which we identified in Chapter 1 emerge, therefore, from these various arguments as key elements of an understanding of the nature of science. They are: an understanding of *the purposes of scientific work*, an understanding of *the nature and status of scientific knowledge* and an understanding of *science as a social enterprise*. Of these, the second is pivotal, with the others drawing to some extent upon it. In Chapter 3, we will review the major strands in philosophical and sociological writings about the nature and status of scientific knowledge in some detail, in order to identify more clearly and specifically the ideas and issues we might explore in students' representations.

3 | Perspectives on the nature of science

| Can we talk of 'understanding the nature of science'?

The absence of consensus

Researching into, or even thinking and talking about, students' understanding of the nature of science immediately raises one important issue: to talk of someone's 'understanding' of something seems to imply that the thing in question is well understood, that there is an agreed 'expert' understanding against which their ideas can be set. This *is* the case when we are considering students' ideas and understandings of science content. If we take, for example, a science domain such as electric circuits, then at the level to which this is studied at school, there is consensus among scientists about the phenomena and about how these should be explained. We might want to treat students' ideas with a certain respect, as prior conceptions or even 'alternative' conceptions rather than misconceptions; but we can use a consensually accepted understanding as a template against which to set students' understandings. The accepted view provides us with a 'map' of the domain.

In contrast, there is less consensus among scholars about the 'nature of science'. Philosophers of science have adopted – and continue to adopt – a range of positions on the major questions and issues about science and scientific knowledge. And it is problematic, at best, to suggest that such views 'progress' or 'approach the truth'. It may reasonably be claimed that scientific knowledge progresses, that we know more now than we used to know about the natural world, but this cannot be so easily claimed of our understanding *of science*. The ideas of today's philosophers of science do not overturn, or subsume, those of earlier writers. Indeed, more recent studies of scientific practice have tended to emphasize the variety, and local contingency, of scientific practices, rather than painting a picture of a general 'method' or 'approach'. So far from clarifying our understanding of the nature of science, or leading towards consensus, their effect has been to broaden the range of views and positions on offer.

Natural sciences

It is important to make clear that we are imposing some limits on this diversity. First, we have chosen to focus on understanding of the nature of science, and not the nature of technology, or of science-and-technology. We would draw the distinction between science and technology largely in terms of purpose, with science seeking to provide explanations of natural events and phenomena, while technology is concerned with the solution of practical problems, drawing on a range of knowledge sources, including science, in reaching acceptable solutions, and sometimes leading to the development of new knowledge (including scientific knowledge) in the process.

Second, throughout this book, 'science' refers to the natural sciences. The boundary between natural and social sciences is not, however, a firm or clearly defined one. There is a longstanding debate about the extent to which there are, or should be, similarities and differences between the methods of the natural and social sciences (see, for example, Bernstein 1976). In broad terms, however, a distinction can be drawn between studies in which the research subjects are conscious beings, whose consciousness could influence (in various ways) the empirical data collected, and studies of inanimate objects (Harré 1972: 188–9). This, however, still leaves a considerable 'grey area', of studies of living creatures (including humans) in situations where it is a matter of debate whether (and if so, to what extent) their consciousness has an effect on the data.

Even within the natural sciences, there is considerable methodological diversity, some of which may have epistemological implications. In many sciences, for instance, experimentation is a key aspect of the process of gaining knowledge. By experiment, we mean a planned intervention, in which a part of the natural world is manipulated in order to obtain data. Some sciences, however, such as astronomy and geology, study objects which cannot be brought into the laboratory and processes which cannot be replicated. Here planned and structured observation often has to take the place of experiment, as a means of testing explanations and predictions (though much experiment may, of course, have been involved in developing the instruments used in these sciences). Also, some sciences seek historical explanations rather than experimental/predictive ones. Gould (1991) argues that palaeontology and evolutionary biology must base their interpretations on the available historical record. The events they study may have happened for contingent reasons, which by their very nature cannot be replicated. The key methodological challenge for such sciences is to legitimate their interpretations of the historical record, since experiment is not an option. Gould's conclusion is that the crucial work in the 'historical' sciences is the detailed *description* of the available evidence.

If differences in subject matter lead to differences in practices, which in turn rest on epistemological differences, perhaps it is more plausible to think of multiple 'natures of sciences'? The very fact, however, that we can recognize and talk about a group of disciplines as natural sciences implies a measure of similarity and family resemblance. Further, since the sciences have quite distinctive (though admittedly in places overlapping) areas of content, some of this similarity resides in shared epistemological and methodological commitments and institutional practices. It is to this common core of ideas about commitments, methods and practices that we refer when talking of 'the nature of science'.

Perspectives on the nature of science: an historical overview

Science is *a body of knowledge* about the natural world; and *a set of practices*, both material and social, which have been used to obtain, and continue to be used to extend, that knowledge. Our grounds for confidence in this body of knowledge and in the efficacy of these practices have exercised philosophers over the centuries. Here we provide only a brief overview of some of the major strands in this ongoing discussion. Fuller accounts may be found in the books by Chalmers (1982), Losee (1972), Newton-Smith (1981) and Gillies (1992).

Explanation in science

The central aim of science is to provide *explanations* for natural phenomena. But what do we mean by an 'explanation'? In one sense, an explanation is simply what is accepted by the person who has given it, and by the person who has received it, as an explanation. We learn from experience what counts as an explanation. One factor crucial to the emergence of science was a shift in the nature of acceptable explanation of events, away from accounts in terms of reasons ('final causes' in Aristotle's terms) to accounts in terms of an observed regularity or an underlying causal model. So, for example, Galileo's understanding of motion depended critically on his decision to ask *how* falling objects fall, rather than *why* they fall. In general, science seeks to exclude teleological explanations, in which a future state of affairs is used to account for events leading up to it.

Various attempts have been made to describe the structure of acceptable explanation in the sciences. One approach is to appeal to the logical structure of an explanation:

an explanation as to *why* things happen, or *why* they are as they are, consists of a statement of an accepted law (or laws) and some other statement(s) relating the particular circumstances to it (or to them) so that from all these the *explicandum* [the thing to be explained] can be deduced.

(Trusted 1987: 52, emphases in original)

For example, imagine we have a syringe containing 100 ml of air at atmospheric pressure. The end of the syringe is sealed. We now push the piston inwards, until the volume of the air is 50 ml, and measure the air pressure. We find it is 2 atmospheres. We can explain this by stating the general law that, for a fixed mass of gas, the pressure is inversely proportional to the volume (Boyle's Law). In this particular case, we have halved the volume. So we can deduce that the pressure should be doubled. The outcome is explained because it is a logical deduction from the general law and the specific starting conditions. This type of explanation is referred to as a Deductive–Nomological (or DN) explanation.

Hempel (1965) provides the classical statement of this view of scientific explanation; an accessible introductory discussion is provided by Trusted (1987). As an account of scientific explanation, the DN model is, however, open to several objections. First, it has difficulty in distinguishing cause and effect clearly: an argument of the same logical structure can explain a storm by a falling barometer and vice versa. Second, as Cartwright (1983: 44–53) points out, science does not, in fact, propose universal generalizations. All generalizations are accompanied by an explicit or implicit *ceteris paribus* clause; that is, they have the qualification 'all other things being equal'. The law is followed under certain special conditions. This means, as Cartwright notes, that they cannot, logically, explain anything, since any departure from the predicted behaviour can always be attributed to the prevailing conditions.

An alternative approach is to emphasize theories, rather than generalizations or laws, as fundamental to explanation in science. A theoretical model describes an imagined world. Events in the real world are then seen as a natural outcome of the behaviour and properties of objects in this imagined world – and hence are 'explained'. Ogborn (1992) proposes a model of explanation as a *history* in a *possible world*. The content of an explanation is 'a set of events in a possible world which lead to what is to be explained, in which that set of events is a possible natural consequence of the nature of the entities in that possible world' (p. 4). He goes on to show the power of this model in providing a structure for considering a wide range of phenomena associated with explanation. This has close similarities to Johnson-Laird's (1983) account of the role of mental models in constructing explanations – allowing ideas to be 'played through' in the imagination to provide a possible account of an observed event.

Theoretical models clearly differ from empirical generalizations (or laws) (though both, as we shall see later, share one important feature: they make claims which go beyond the data on which they are based). Many laws, however, are underpinned by theoretical models. So, for example, in the example above of compressing a gas, Boyle's Law is supported by a theoretical model (the kinetic theory of gases) in which pressure is interpreted in terms of collisions between molecules of the gas and the walls of the container. The presence of such a model in the background is, however, irrelevant to the logical form of a DN explanation. And many quite acceptable explanations remain at the level of the empirical law, even when there is an underlying theoretical model. For example, if someone asks 'why is the handle of a saucepan made of plastic and not of metal, like the rest of the pan?', then the answer 'because plastics are poor conductors of heat' would normally be taken as an explanation. There would not normally be a perceived need to go on to explain free electron models of thermal conduction in metals and the different atomic/molecular structure of insulators in order to explain satisfactorily the choice of plastic as the handle material.

There are also quite striking differences in kind among theoretical models (for a fuller discussion, see Harré 1972). Some, like the kinetic theory of matter, introduce unobservable objects such as atoms and molecules, with distinctive properties like constant motion with an average speed related to the temperature. Other theoretical models, such as the germ theory of disease, give a key role to objects which are not observable with the naked eye, but which can be observed using instruments, in this case microscopes. Some theories, like the heliocentric model of the solar system or the plate tectonic model of the evolution of the Earth's surface, introduce no new unobservable objects, but seem much more like a description of the system, from a particular viewpoint, or over a longer time-span than human lives. Yet others propose formal entities such as force or energy, which are not, in principle, observable, but provide one means (though not necessarily the only means) of structuring phenomena and events. The unifying characteristic of theories is that they provide a mental model; by 'running' the model in the mind, predictions can be made and explanations given. Some models can be expressed mathematically, allowing the behaviour of more complex situations and systems to be simulated and predicted.

Observation first: the inductive view

If science aims to provide explanations for phenomena and events, then perhaps the central question to be asked about science as a knowledge form is: why should we have confidence in the scientific account? What is it about the scientific approach which enables it to provide 'reliable knowledge' (Ziman 1978)? For Chalmers (1982: 1), the 'widely held common-sense view of science' is that:

> Scientific knowledge is proven knowledge. Scientific theories are derived in some rigorous way from the facts of experience acquired

by observation and experiment. Science is based on what we can see and hear and touch, etc.

This is both an *empiricist* and an *inductive* view. *Empiricism* is the view that secure knowledge is that which comes directly from experience. *Induction* is the process of inferring generalizations from a series of specific (or *singular*) observations. Examples might include the statement that 'the sun rises every morning in the east', based upon the repeated observation that, every morning so far, it has done so; or proposing that 'all non-metals are electrical insulators' on the basis of tests carried out on a collection of metallic and non-metallic specimens. Although the idea of induction dates back at least to Aristotle (Losee 1972: 8), the claim that induction is distinctively the 'method' of science is most closely associated with Francis Bacon (1561–1626). Philosophers, however, have long been aware (Losee 1972: 31ff.) of a fundamental problem about induction: unlike deductive reasoning, where we start from a set of initial propositions and use logical rules of argument to reach a conclusion (so that, if the premises are sound, then the conclusion *must* be valid), we can never be completely sure that an inductive generalization is true. The next singular observation we make may show that it is false. The second example above is a case in point. If we now add graphite to our collection of materials, we discover a non-metal which is not an electrical insulator. The generalization 'all non-metals are electrical insulators' is seen to be false. A first response to this objection might be to argue that, provided sufficient observations have been made, covering a sufficiently wide range of situations and cases, then we can be confident that a generalization is valid. But that begs the question of how many is 'sufficient', or what a 'sufficiently wide range' might be. We have to accept that, if scientific generalizations are arrived at through inductive reasoning, then it cannot be logically demonstrated that they are true. By the same reasoning, theoretical models, if they are derived inductively from experience, can never be shown to be true.

Philosophers have responded to this in a variety of ways. In the eighteenth century, David Hume's analysis of induction led him to conclude that generalizations can have no logical basis in singular pieces of evidence (Ayer 1981). Hume conceded, however, that humans do indeed think in these ways; he acknowledged that he, himself, did so when 'out of his study'. This he regarded as a 'habit of the mind' – a psychological propensity rather than a logical step. Hume was prepared to accept that induction was, indeed, the method of the sciences; but he argued that it was grounded in human psychology rather than in logic.

For many philosophers, however, this is an uncomfortable conclusion. J.S. Mill (1803–1873) developed a logic of experimentation based on four 'methods', of which the most important were the Method of Agreement and the Method of Difference (Mill 1843, in Brown *et al.* 1981: 76–82). The former involves listing instances in which a particular phenomenon occurs, and then searching for common factors associated with each of these instances. If one can be found, then this suggests, according to Mill, that it is probable that this is the cause of the phenomenon. The Method of Difference involves listing instances and non-instances of a phenomenon and then looking for a factor which is present when the phenomenon occurs, but absent when it does not. Mill's arguments did not, however, allay concerns about the inductive method; these methods may underlie much practical reasoning, but they do not lead to results which must, logically, follow. They do not, therefore, provide any assurance that the inductive method leads to true generalizations or laws.

The American philosopher, C.S. Pierce, a contemporary of Mill, introduced the term 'abduction' for the process of working back from observation to an account of an underlying model or principle which could account for what was observed. He acknowledged that there was no 'method' for doing so, but that the process involved creativity and imagination. Most empiricists would now share this view, that there is no automatic, or algorithmic, method of deriving a generalization or theoretical model from a set of singular observations; modern empiricists would argue that, however the generalization or theory comes to be proposed, our grounds for confidence in it lie in the set of singular observations which underpin it (van Fraassen 1980).

In the twentieth century, inductive reasoning has been taken up and developed by the philosophical movement known as 'logical positivism' (Ayer 1946). Logical positivists argue that the aim of philosophy is not to establish which propositions are true or false, but to clarify the meaning of statements. Some are *analytic*: they follow logically from previous assumptions but, since they are logically entailed by those assumptions, do not tell us anything new about the world. Others, including all scientific statements, are *synthetic*: they propose a link between two or more things which are not necessarily (i.e logically and inevitably) related in this way. Such statements must be verifiable by observation, at least in principle. All other statements, according to the logical positivists, are non-sensical and meaningless – that is, literally 'without meaning'. The logical positivist view of synthetic statements, and hence of scientific knowledge, is an inductive one, with a particular emphasis on verifiability and observation.

While accepting the logical problem of induction, logical positivists (Carnap 1950) have claimed, using arguments based on formal logic and the mathematics of probability, that induction can lead, logically, to generalizations which are *probably* true, and that additional observations can increase this probability. Against such claims, it is usually argued that, however many singular observations are made, the ratio:

$$\frac{\text{number of actual observations made}}{\text{number of situations to which the generalization applies}}$$

is always zero for universal generalizations, as these claim to apply to *all* possible cases. So the probability that the generalization is true remains zero.

The problem of induction solved? Popper and falsification

Against the background of logical positivism, Karl Popper (1934) produced his now classic critique of induction. Popper argues that induction cannot be shown to lead logically to true generalizations, or even to ones which are 'probably true'. Unlike Hume, however, he does not resolve the problem this creates for philosophy of science by appealing to 'habits of the mind'. Instead, he argues that induction is *not* the method of science. Science, Popper claims, is the method of conjectures and refutations – a 'hypothetico-deductive' approach. Science progresses by proposing testable hypotheses; these are then subjected to rigorous tests in which predictions deduced from the hypothesis are compared with observation *with a view to falsifying the hypothesis*[1]. Unlike verification, which is impossible (as no finite number of observations can *prove* that a generalization is true), a single observation which conflicts with a generalization can, logically, falsify it. Popper's example is the statement 'All swans are white', which cannot be proved by any number of observations of white swans, but can be falsified by one observation of a non-white swan.

Popper argues that science makes progress through the replacement of hypotheses by newer ones with greater empirical content; that is, they account for a larger number of observations. The stimulus to such progress is the realization that current hypotheses are deficient and this can only come through their falsification. So the aim of experimental tests is the falsification of hypotheses. The key criterion that a hypothesis must meet to be called 'scientific' is that it has testable consequences which could lead, in principle, to its falsification. If it is stated in such terms that no conceivable observation could ever falsify it, then it is not, for Popper, scientific.

Another important consequence of Popper's approach is to separate the process of conceiving of a scientific idea from that of justifying it. The former involves the proposing of bold conjectures which account for known data and lead to testable consequences. According to Popper, there is little that we can say about this process; a novel theory or hypothesis is a creative product of an individual mind and there is no pattern in the way these arise. The latter involves severe testing with a view to falsification. The 'method of science' does not lie in the way new ideas are conceived but, rather, in the rigorous and systematic way such ideas are tested.

There are, however, a number of problems with this falsificationist view. First, the view that all experimentation is carried out within a hypothetico-deductive context seems somewhat narrow, and to make too many assumptions about the branch of science one is thinking about and its stage of development. It seems clear, for example, that when scientists undertake an initial exploration of a new area, their primary concern is often simply to collect data and information about the area. They have no theory in mind as they probe, and their data-gathering cannot convincingly be portrayed as theory-testing (see, Hacking, 1983, especially chapter 10). And in the specific context of this book, it may be important to note that, for most school students, a significant proportion of their first-hand experience of science (on which their image of scientific practice and purposes is substantially based) more closely resembles scientists' initial explorations of an area than the more mature exploration of an established field, guided by an agreed theory.

Second, the strong emphasis on falsification as an aim does not ring true of actual scientific practice. As Lakatos is once said to have remarked: 'You know a scientist who wants to falsify his theory?' (Newton-Smith 1981: 52). If a scientist undertakes experimental work in order to test a hypothesis, the intention (and the hope) is invariably to corroborate it rather than to falsify it. This is not simply a reflection of the natural human desire to be right rather than wrong; many of the episodes in science which are celebrated as 'crucial' experiments are verifications rather than falsifications. Eddington's measurements of the deflection of light from stars during a solar eclipse, which corroborated the predictions of Einstein's general theory of relativity, and Fresnel's observation of the bright spot at the centre of the shadow of a disc, are just two examples. In general, few scientific investigations appear to be undertaken in the hope of falsifying a hypothesis.

A second line of criticism centres on the absence of any obvious place for the notion of 'truth' in the hypothetico-deductive approach. If induction is logically invalid, and hypotheses are bold conjectures, then we can never have grounds for believing any conjecture to be 'true'. It is, at best, 'not yet falsified'. So what is the purpose of science, if we cannot attain the truth (or, more precisely, we cannot ever be sure if we have attained it)? Popper's answer is that theories can have differing degrees of *verisimilitude*, or 'nearness to the truth'. We can compare the relative verisimilitude of theories and so can claim that science makes progress. His argument, however, has been subjected to significant criticism, along lines similar to those used against probabilistic interpretations of induction (for a fuller discussion, see Newton-Smith 1981: chapter 3).

Observation is theory-laden

A serious challenge both to the falsificationist approach and to induction is the argument that all observation is theory-laden. Hanson (1958) uses a series of examples to show how the reports people give of what they see presuppose theories of different sorts, and concludes:

> There is a sense, then, in which seeing is a 'theory-laden' undertaking. Observation of x is shaped by prior knowledge of x. Another influence on observation rests in the language or notation used to express what we know, and without which there would be little we could recognise as knowledge.
>
> (Hanson 1958: 146)

In the context of science teaching, we might see this 'theory-ladenness' of observation in pupils' drawings of what they observe when using a microscope to look at cells; those who have seen textbook diagrams of cells produce very different drawings from those who have not (Hainsworth 1956). Similarly, if pupils are asked to map a magnetic field using iron filings and sketch what they observe, their drawings differ according to the prior knowledge of magnetic field patterns which they bring to the task (Gott and Welford 1987).

If the theory-ladenness of all observation is accepted, then the basic empiricist idea that we can have secure knowledge based upon sense experience is overturned. Even observation statements depend on, and are infected by, the theoretical commitments of the observer. There is no 'pure' bedrock of observable 'fact'. The inductive view, which begins with observation, is seriously compromised. Recognizing this, logical positivists have tried to argue that there *is* a clear observational–theoretical distinction (Carnap 1966). Falsificationism is equally challenged, since it depends on the idea that hypotheses can be tested by comparing predictions based upon them with observation. But these observations themselves incorporate theoretical ideas. So a conflict between a prediction and an observation statement may be attributed to a problem with the theory (or theories) which are implicit in the observation statement itself, and not with the hypothesis being tested. As a result, falsification can never be clear-cut.

Popper himself accepted this argument and proposed that all statements, even 'basic statements' reporting an observation, should be seen as conjectural. They may be consensually accepted as a basis for theory-testing, but this is ultimately a *decision* made by the scientific community (see Newton-Smith 1981: 59–64). Feyerabend talks of 'quickly decidable sentences' (quoted in Maxwell 1962: 13) – statements which can readily be agreed by all concerned. Newton-Smith (1981: 28) argues that:

> while we cannot have absolute faith in any particular report ... we are entitled to have general faith in the low-level O-reports [observational reports] we are inclined to make. Our success in coping with the world gives us grounds for this general confidence. If such judgments were not by and large reliable, we should not be still here to make judgments.

Others (Maxwell 1962; Putnam 1962; Shapere 1982) have similarly argued that there is a continuum from the less to the more theoretical, and that any line drawn to divide this into two categories is necessarily arbitrary. While a rigid distinction cannot be made between statements which are 'purely observational' and others which contain theoretical terms and ideas, statements can differ in the amount of theoretical 'baggage' they carry. Finally, it is important to note that, while an observation statement may be theory-laden, it is not necessarily laden with the theory which it is being used to test.

For all these reasons, the distinction between observation and theory remains a useful one, despite the acknowledged difficulties in drawing any clear line between observation statements and theoretical ones.

From theories to research programmes

The criticisms of the naive falsificationist position outlined above led some philosophers to develop more sophisticated forms of falsificationism. The best known of these is in the work of Imre Lakatos (1970, 1978), who argues that it is misleading to represent the scientific process as involving 'a two-cornered fight between theory and experiment'. Instead, 'history of science suggests that (1) tests are – at least – three-cornered fights between rival theories and experiments and (2) some of the most interesting experiments result, *prima facie*, in confirmation rather than falsification' (Lakatos 1978: 31). Lakatos acknowledges that scientists do not reject a theory just because an observation has been reported which apparently falsifies it. Even if the observation is accepted as valid, they will hold on to the theory, often hoping that some modification or new piece of information will turn up which will reconcile the theory and the apparently anomalous observation. In short, theories are never rejected unless a plausible alternative theory is available. For Lakatos the issue then becomes the process by which rival theories are compared.

He develops his arguments around the central notion of a 'research programme'. This has a 'hard core' of basic assumptions, which must not be modified or rejected. Around this, there is a 'protective belt' of auxiliary hypotheses and theories, relating to such matters as initial conditions, how instruments work, and so on. The stipulation that the hard core cannot be changed, even in the light of apparent anomalies, Lakatos calls the 'negative heuristic' of a research programme. The 'positive heuristic' is a set of loose guidelines on how the research programme might develop in the face of anomalies. Lakatos then argues that research programmes can be either 'progressive' or 'degenerating', depending on whether they predict new and interesting phenomena which are subsequently observed, or simply provide *ad hoc* (and *post hoc*) accounts of observations. Popper was similarly critical of *ad hoc* adjustments to theories to account for anomalous observations, but Lakatos sets this in the context of research programmes rather than single theories.

Using this framework of ideas, Lakatos attempts to show how certain theory choices in the history of science can be portrayed as rational – based on the weight of evidence and on reason, rather than whim. His approach, however, has been criticized as providing only a rationalization of theory choice after the event, but providing no guidance to scientists facing such theory choices in the present. Lakatos's criteria for theory choice are so general that they cannot be applied in actual situations of theory choice. Hence Feyerabend (1970: 215) refers to Lakatos's method as 'a verbal ornament'. Feyerabend's own solution is to argue that there is no 'method of science' or rule for deciding between rival theories:

The idea that science can, and should, be run according to fixed and universal rules is both unrealistic and pernicious . . . All methodologies have their limitations and the only 'rule' that survives is 'anything goes'.

(Feyerabend 1975: 295–6)

Another influential view which agrees with Lakatos in rejecting the notion that a theory can ever be tested in isolation is the so-called Duhem–Quine thesis. Duhem's original argument was that an experiment in physics can never test an isolated hypothesis but only a group of hypotheses:

the physicist can never subject an isolated hypothesis to experimental test; when the experiment is in disagreement with the predictions, what he learns is that at least one of the hypotheses constituting this group is unacceptable and ought to be modified; but the experiment does not designate which one should be changed.

(Duhem 1904/5, cited in Gillies 1992: 98–9)

Hence, any anomaly can be dealt with in a large number of ways. It will certainly not necessarily lead to rejection of a core theory. While Duhem explicitly limited the scope of this idea to physics, and considered that it did not apply to several of the other sciences, Quine proposed that it can apply quite generally, to all statements. He argues that 'any statement can be held true come what may, if we make drastic enough adjustments elsewhere in the system' (Quine 1951: 43).

Letting history speak: Kuhn's revolution

The publication of Thomas Kuhn's *The Structure of Scientific Revolutions* (1962) itself caused a revolution in thinking about science. Kuhn's basic thesis appears innocuous enough: that we should pay more dispassionate attention to the details of the history of science in theorizing about the nature of science and the progress of scientific ideas. On the basis of historical studies, Kuhn proposes two distinct types of scientific activity. One he calls 'normal science'. This is the kind of science practised by most scientists most of the time. It involves working within existing frameworks of theory and practice, articulating the implications and working out further applications of the accepted theoretical ideas in that branch of science. Kuhn refers to this activity, somewhat provocatively, as 'puzzle-solving'. From time to time, however, anomalous results may begin to accumulate in a branch of scientific activity. If it is impossible to accommodate these within the current theoretical framework, they will precipitate a crisis in the field. This is eventually resolved when an alternative theory emerges and is accepted by the community of practitioners in the field. This change, which can occur over a relatively short period, Kuhn calls a 'scientific revolution'. Following the revolution a new normal scientific tradition takes over.

In the account above, we have deliberately avoided using the term 'paradigm' which plays a key role in Kuhn's book. The reason is that Kuhn has been criticized for having used the term in a wide variety of different senses (Masterman 1970), to the extent that its meaning is unclear. Kuhn acknowledges the force of this criticism and attempts in a later book (Kuhn 1977) to clarify his intentions. He argues that the key sense of 'paradigm' is its original one: a concrete exemplar of a practice, or problem solution. Individuals learn how to practise science in any given field, he argues, by learning the paradigms which guide practice in that field. For the network of facts, laws, theories and practices shared by the scientists who work in a given field, Kuhn suggests the term 'disciplinary matrix'. (Some social scientists, however, have continued to use 'paradigm' for this wider set of commitments.) In Kuhn's (1977) terminology, a scientific revolution is the period between the dominance of an old disciplinary matrix and a new one.

The aspect of Kuhn's ideas which caused controversy was his account of scientific revolutions. Kuhn likens the change to a 'gestalt switch' – a new disciplinary matrix represents a new way of looking at the world. He argues that the old and the new views cannot be compared directly. They may even be incommensurable; that is, the same terms can have quite different meanings within the two systems of thinking. A crisis in a field of science is resolved, in the final analysis, by a decision of the scientific community of workers in that field: 'What better criterion [for theory choice] than the decision of the scientific group could there be?' Kuhn asks (1970: 170). As critics were quick to point out, this makes theory choice seem 'a matter of mob psychology' (Lakatos 1970: 178). Another consequence of Kuhn's position is that a change of disciplinary matrix does not necessarily represent 'progress' and certainly not progress *towards* anything.

In response to these criticisms, Kuhn (1977: 321–2) identifies five 'characteristics of a good scientific theory':

1 A theory should be accurate within its domain, that is, consequences deducible from a theory should be in demonstrated agreement with the results of existing experiments and observations.
2 A theory should be consistent, not only internally or with itself, but also with other currently accepted theories applicable to related aspects of nature.
3 It should have broad scope: in particular, a theory's consequences should extend far beyond the particular observations, laws or sub-theories it was initially designed to explain.
4 It should be simple, bringing order to phenomena that in its absence would be individually isolated and, as a set, confused.
5 A theory should be fruitful of new research findings: that is, it should disclose new phenomena or previously unnoted relationships among those already known.

These 'standard criteria ... together with others of much the same sort, ... provide *the* shared basis for theory choice' (Kuhn 1977: 322, emphasis in original). This seems scarcely radical. All Kuhn appears to be arguing is the unexceptionable position that there is no algorithm for applying these (and similar) criteria to any given case, or for determining the relative weight to be given to each if they point towards different conclusions. Those who argue that theory choice is based on rational criteria, such as Popper, Lakatos and Laudan (1977), would agree. Kuhn chooses, however, to maintain a non-rationalist stance, by arguing that these criteria cannot be rationally justified but are simply the generally accepted ones. In practical terms, however, there seems little difference between these positions, with terms like 'rational' and 'irrational' used primarily as a rhetoric of approbation or denigration.

The 'sociological turn'

Kuhn's emphasis on the scientific community as the arbiter of change was quickly seized upon by sociologists, who saw it as opening up the possibility of a sociology of scientific knowledge (SSK). The idea of a 'sociology of knowledge' was first developed in a systematic way by Karl Mannheim (see, for example, Mulkay 1979: 10–17). Mannheim, however, saw scientific knowledge as lying outside the scope of sociological explanation. While a sociological account of scientific error might be produced, accepted (or true) scientific knowledge was not, in Mannheim's view, open to a sociological account. In the 1970s, several groups of sociologists began to challenge this position. The so-called 'strong programme' in the sociology of scientific knowledge (Bloor 1976) is based on the premise that a symmetrical approach should be adopted in accounting for both the successes and failures of science. It is, in Bloor's view, unacceptable to apply one set of criteria and arguments in accounting for scientific ideas which later came to be seen as erroneous, and a different set for those which have come to be accepted. According to Bloor (1976: 4–5):

> The sociology of scientific knowledge should adhere to the following four tenets . . . :
>
> 1 It would be causal, that is, concerned with the conditions which bring about belief or states of knowledge. Naturally there will be other types of causes apart from social ones which will co-operate in bringing about belief.
> 2 It would be impartial with respect to truth or falsity, rationality or irrationality, success or failure. Both sides of these dichotomies will require explanation.
> 3 It would be symmetrical in its style of explanation. The same types of cause would explain, say, true and false beliefs.
> 4 It would be reflexive. In principle, its patterns of explanation would have to be applicable to sociology itself.

Note the emphasis, in Bloor's first tenet, on causes. Sociology, as a science, is interested in the *causes* of beliefs – with, as Bloor puts it, 'the conditions which bring about belief or states of knowledge'. This contrasts with the philosopher's focus on the *rationality* of beliefs or knowledge, which is an essentially different project.

In line with Bloor's second and third tenets, SSK has embraced a *relativist* methodology. Relativism denies that things are true or false in virtue of an independent reality. Things can only be true or false for a particular group at a certain time – that is all the terms 'true' and 'false' can mean. So studies have presented evidence to support their argument that specific pieces of scientific knowledge (including currently accepted ideas, on an equal footing with ideas now seen as erroneous) are socially constructed and negotiated, and can be attributed to the interests, or the location within social groupings, of the scientists involved (Barnes and Shapin 1979; Collins 1981a). One important influence on the development of SSK was anthropological studies which provided examples of viable and coherent belief systems based upon alternative accounts of the natural order, yet able to operate successfully at the practical level (see Giere 1988: 50–61; Gjertsen 1989: 234–257). Acknowledging limits to the possible extent of variation in viable accounts of the world, one leading practitioner of SSK has argued that 'sociologists as a whole would acknowledge that the world in some way constrains what is believed to be' (Barnes 1974: vii). Collins (1981b: 54) counters this with a methodological principle which he sees as central to SSK: 'the appropriate attitude for conducting this kind of enquiry is to assume that "the natural world in no way constrains what is believed to be"'. This, it should be noted, is proposed as a *methodological principle* to guide sociological work, and not (necessarily) as an epistemological position.

Critics have questioned the success of studies carried out within SSK in showing exactly how specific scientific ideas have been caused by specific social factors (see, for example, Chalmers 1990: 80–114). Collins and Cox (1976) respond by challenging the critics of SSK to show in detail, in specific cases, precisely how the natural world causes specific pieces of scientific knowledge to be held as such. The variety of views about the natural world which have been held by different societies undermines, they suggest, the claim that the natural world 'compels' any particular interpretation of it.

Later developments of the sociological programme have included richly detailed accounts of everyday life in scientific research laboratories, with a focus on the social interactions involved and the processes by which outputs (mainly in the form of texts) are produced and transformed as they pass into wider circulation (Latour and Woolgar 1979; Lynch 1985). Others have focused on scientists' discourse and on the ways in which different types of account are used in different social situations (Gilbert and Mulkay 1984; Mulkay 1985).

As a result of the work of sociologists, the idea that scientific knowledge is, in some sense, 'socially constructed', is one which has passed into widespread use. [The term has resonances with the title of Berger and

Luckmann's (1967) influential book, *The Social Construction of Reality*. Berger and Luckmann, however, were writing quite explicitly of 'social reality', which they contrast with natural reality.] It is sometimes difficult to be sure exactly what is meant by the claim that scientific knowledge is socially constructed. One version is unproblematical and can be readily conceded. This is the argument that decisions about which areas of scientific enquiry should be pursued (and supported with funds) are based on factors external to science. Clearly, the interests of agencies external to science, notably the military and industry, have ensured that certain branches of science are more developed than others. As a result, the corpus of knowledge we recognize as science is, it can reasonably be argued, a consequence of social pressures. Under different conditions we would have some pieces of knowledge we do not now possess, and some which we do have would be unknown.

A stronger argument, and one which raises much more fundamental issues, is that the *contents* of accepted science are socially constructed. This is the core argument of SSK. In one sense this, too, can be readily accepted. The process by which a knowledge claim from an individual scientist or research group is transmuted into 'scientific knowledge' involves a peer review process within which the controls on publication of findings are central. A knowledge claim can only become 'knowledge' through an institutionalized, and hence social, process. But rather more than this is usually intended by the claim that the content of accepted science is socially constructed. The key issue, which is still strongly disputed, is whether it is the social processes affecting the relevant scientific community, or features of the natural world, which are the principal determinant of scientific knowledge. As Giere (1988: 55–6) puts it: 'The real issue is the extent to which, and by what means, nature constrains scientific theorizing'.

In reflecting on this issue, it may be important to recognize that the physical sciences are the 'hard case' for SSK. If we are thinking instead of a science such as ethology, or social biology, then it is much easier to concede that researchers' interests and social locations may influence their observations and interpretations. Thus, for instance, it has been claimed that scientific work on the social behaviour of chimpanzees is influenced by the gender of the researchers. Longino (1990) provides an interesting discussion of a number of such cases, arguing for the influence of social factors on scientific knowledge but stopping short of a complete relativism.

Realism and instrumentalism

The ways in which philosophers and sociologists talk about science is so different from the way the enterprise is experienced by working scientists that some have been led to question whether they are referring to the same thing. While insiders' accounts cannot be taken as specially privileged – indeed Lakatos is said to have remarked that a practising scientist has as much need of philosophy as a fish of hydrodynamics – it is a matter of some concern if philosophical accounts of science differ radically from those of thoughtful practitioners (Polanyi 1958; Ziman 1967, 1978).

Scientists' views of science are usually characterized by an unproblematic, commonsense realism; science is taken to be an attempt to obtain knowledge of a real, physical, external world, which behaves as it does quite independently of our views about it. This does not, of course, imply the possibility of certain knowledge; we can have, at best, fallible knowledge of this real world. Ogborn (1994) argues that the success of science in producing consensually agreed knowledge of aspects of the natural world is a contingent historical fact, which could not have been guaranteed at the outset, and is the result of sustained *work*. In major part, it is a consequence of the 'decision' of scientists to limit their areas of interest to questions about which such consensus is obtainable.

The alternative to realism is instrumentalism, the view that theories are simply tools for thinking. They are useful if they lead to predictions which are borne out by observation and experience. But there is no claim that the entities and processes they talk about correspond to anything in the world.

Realists argue that, while we can entertain any ideas we want about the natural world, only certain ideas enable us to *act* successfully. Our ideas about the world are sustained not through thinking about it, but by acting in it. Bhaskar (1978) distinguishes the transitive nature of thought, in which any idea can be sustained, from the intransitive nature of the world, which, by behaving simply as it does, and not in accordance with our wishes, sustains some ideas but not others. Hacking (1983) tells how he became persuaded that electrons are real through his conversations with scientists who talked of 'spraying electrons' at targets. It was their ability to *do things* with electrons which made them real.

Newton-Smith (1981: 21) proposes that the fundamental claim of realism is that theoretical statements in science are either true or false, and which they are depends on how the world is, independently of us. Harré (1986), however, argues that we can never tell whether any theoretical statement is true or false, so a defence of this version of realism is hopeless. He proposes instead a 'referential realism', based on the argument that we have good reason to believe that 'many of the referring expressions that occur in theoretical discourses have referents in the world that exist independently of human cognitive and practical activity' (p. 191). That is, there are good grounds for believing that many of the things of which theories speak correspond to things which exist in the world independently of our theorizing about them.

Hacking makes a distinction between *realism about entities* and *realism about theories*. An example might help to clarify this distinction. A theory of the structure of the atom might propose various things about the smaller objects out of which an atom is 'made' and how these interact. It is possible to be realist about the atom as an entity (to accept that there really are atoms) without necessarily accepting as true the theoretical account of the atom's structure. This could be regarded, quite consistently, as largely instrumental – simply leading to good predictions. Hacking (1983: 28–9) argues for a realism about both entities and theories, though on slightly different grounds for each. Cartwright (1983), on the other hand, argues for a realism about entities but not about theories.

As we have noted, at the core of several recent realist arguments is an emphasis on action, as opposed to mere talk. Ogborn (1994) links this argument to Piaget's claim that the child's conception of objects, of space and time is constructed through action on the world, and the internalization of these actions. Hence scientific thinking, and the kind of provisional 'certainty' about things to which it can lead, are seen as a natural development of commonsense thinking.

Post-modernist developments

A current strand of thought about the nature of science calls into question the status of the knowledge of scientific experts in comparison to that of other members of the public. Studies of scientific knowledge used for specific social purposes (e.g. Layton *et al.* 1993) are challenging the image of scientific knowledge as a universal and privileged 'given'. Instead, they portray local knowledges developed to address specific needs and interests in specific social contexts and raise the question of whose knowledge has the right to be labelled as 'science'. Commenting on the views of participants in their case studies, Layton *et al.* (1993: 138–9) remark:

> Those in the case studies who sought to use scientific knowledge to ground the actions they wished to take found themselves, like many post-modernists, questioning much of what was presented as 'given' and discovering that, in some cases, e.g. estimates of risk, scientific 'facts' involve a large element of social construction/subjectivity and/ or were related to circumstances far removed from those in which they conducted their daily lives (e.g. the management of an energy budget).

Rather than seeing science as an endeavour to establish claims about a world which exists independently of the knower, such a post-modernist perspective adopts a view of local knowledges being established within particular situations or standpoints. The perspective can perhaps be seen to embrace a view of knowledge in action but from an instrumentalist rather than a realist position. It is not proposing total relativism in relation to the truth of scientific knowledge claims, but rather that scientific knowledge claims are limited in scope by the physical and social settings to which the knowledge is related.

| Implications for a research study

It is apparent from the overview presented above that perspectives on the nature of science are both diverse and complex. What, then, can we take from these ideas to inform a study of school students' understandings of the nature of science? At the end of Chapter 2 we identified three strands, or features, of this understanding. In the light of the arguments and issues outlined in this chapter, we can now move towards a clearer definition of each of these strands, identifying some of the features of knowledge about science which might guide our enquiries with students. This is set out below, taking each of the three features in turn. The outcome is not a normative template against which to set students' ideas, but a 'map' to guide the design of an exploratory study. We will return to this 'map' in Chapter 5, where we identify specific research questions and outline the approach we adopted to probe these aspects of students' reasoning.

An understanding of the purposes of scientific work

Early in this chapter, we discussed briefly the difference between science and technology, seeing this in terms of the aims of the two enterprises. We also outlined a distinction between the natural and social sciences in terms of their subject matter. While recognizing that neither of these demarcations is unproblematic when considered in more detail, there is broad agreement about the purpose of scientific work at the level which we might reasonably expect in school students' reasoning. Understandings we might expect students to hold include:

- Natural science addresses questions about the natural world. Its aim is to *explain* natural phenomena.
- Science considers questions about both inanimate and animate objects, but excludes those where the consciousness of the objects of study might be expected to influence appreciably the data collected. It also excludes questions which involve values (about what 'should' or 'ought to' happen), or opinions.

More sophisticated ideas which might be reflected in some students' reasoning include the Popperian notion of 'falsifiability' as a criterion for regarding a proposition as 'scientific', and hence that the aim of science is to propose hypotheses which are falsifiable. This would not, however, be universally agreed as a criterion for demarcating the scientific from the non-scientific or pseudo-scientific.

An understanding of the nature and status of scientific knowledge

Much of this chapter has been concerned with ideas about scientific knowledge. It is tempting to see the chronological account presented as a record of 'progress' towards an ever better understanding of the nature of scientific knowledge. While it is true that some positions, such as logical positivism, have been largely abandoned in the face of criticism, it is difficult to argue that any single position provides an adequate account of the development of scientific knowledge *in general*, or of our grounds for confidence in it. The claim, for example, that scientific enquiry is essentially hypothetico-deductive in structure, and that a hypothetico-deductive understanding of science is therefore 'better' than an inductive one, seems an over-simplification. It may appear to account better for some specific cases or instances, but to fit others less well. Similarly, the notion that empirical enquiry in science always takes the form of an experiment, designed to test predictions based upon theory, over-emphasizes one variety of scientific work, carried out in well-developed fields of enquiry, in one type of science. The absence of consensus about any single model of scientific enquiry does not, of course, mean that all positions are equally valid. We are not arguing for a complete relativism. Rather, we are suggesting that the diversity of accounts suggests that any interpretation must be viewed *in context*, in relation to specific examples of scientific work or enquiry.

Two major issues discussed above, about the rationality or non-rationality of theory choice and the realist or instrumentalist interpretation of theories, are unresolved and probably unresolvable. Neither position on these issues can be regarded as more 'advanced' or more 'sophisticated' than the alternative. The realism/instrumentalism issue seems a particularly difficult one to probe in students' thinking.

Within the diversity of views, we would suggest that the following ideas command broad consensus and might usefully be explored in a study of students' understanding:

- Scientific enquiry involves the collection and use of data (evidence). This may be used to provide the 'raw material' which an explanation has to account for; or to test proposed explanations. [Clearly, the argument that all observations are theory-laden challenges any simple distinction between data and explanation. Even so, for the reasons given earlier in the chapter, we believe that a useful and viable distinction can be made between statements which are more closely tied to observation (and hence more readily agreed by all concerned) and those which are more remote from observation and hence more conjectural.]
- Scientific explanations are based upon generalizations (laws) and theoretical models (theories).
- Laws and theories are always underdetermined by data. That is, proposing a law or a theory always involves going beyond the available data. So they are inevitably conjectural.
- Choices between competing theories are based on criteria such as accuracy of prediction, consistency both internally and with data, breadth of scope, simplicity and fruitfulness in suggesting lines of enquiry. Judgement is, however, involved in deciding how these apply to any given case.

An understanding of science as a social enterprise

Simple descriptive accounts of the social organization of the scientific community, of the mechanisms of funding of scientific work and of the processes of publication and dissemination of findings, raise few contentious issues. We would be interested in any ideas school students have about these matters, but would not see significant critical issues to explore more actively. Most, if not all, of the positions reviewed in this chapter would agree that:

• Scientific knowledge is the product of a *community*, not of an individual. Findings reported by an individual must survive an institutional checking and testing mechanism, before being accepted as knowledge.

It would therefore be of interest to see whether this idea forms part of students' thinking. Where there is much less agreement is about the relative importance of social factors, as compared with natural ones, in establishing scientific knowledge – the 'social construction of scientific knowledge' argument. Here it might be of interest to explore students' views about the reasons for disagreement about controversial issues in science, or in the application of science, with a view to documenting the ideas and arguments used, while acknowledging the absence of any normative standard against which to set these views.

| Notes

1 In this discussion of Popper's ideas, we use the term 'hypothesis' to cover both 'generalization' and 'theory'. Popper's example of the black swan involves a universal generalization. Popper (1959: 59) writes that 'scientific theories are universal statements', and couches most of his discussion in terms of 'singular statements' and 'universal statements'. Earlier in this chapter, we drew a distinction between laws (generalizations) and theories (models). It seems clear, however, that Popper does not see his argument as depending upon any distinction between the two but as applying equally to both.

4 | What do we already know about students' understanding of the nature of science?

In this chapter, we describe and discuss some previous studies of students' ideas about the nature of science. Our aim is not to provide a comprehensive review of research carried out in this area; for this, the reader is referred to Ledermann (1992) and Arnold and Millar (1993). Rather, our intention is to consider the research strategies used and the findings reported in those research studies which have most directly influenced our own thinking about young people's understanding of the nature of science.

In Chapters 1–3, we have identified three features of students' representations of the nature of science on which to focus attention: students' views on *the purpose of scientific work*, their understanding of *the nature and status of scientific knowledge*, and their understanding of *science as a social enterprise*. We will therefore review and discuss critically the findings of previous research studies under these three headings. This may help to clarify the extent of our existing knowledge of students' understandings of the nature of science, to identify any aspects of that knowledge about which little is known. We shall also consider the range and appropriateness of methods which have been used to probe students' understandings.

In evaluating reported findings, it is important to recognize that students' ideas about the nature of science are likely to be influenced by a range of factors. School-age students are unlikely to have direct experience of the workings of scientific communities, but will almost certainly have been exposed to images of science and scientists in the media, through conversations with adults and peers, and through the images of science portrayed both explicitly and implicitly in school science lessons. Their knowledge of 'real science' is second-hand and indirect, often mediated by other interests; their knowledge of 'school science' is immediate and direct. So it may be important to know whether students, as they respond to a question or task given by researchers, are thinking about the work of scientists and the scientific community, as they understand it, or about their own experience of 'doing science' in school. There is no reason to assume that their views of these two activities are the same, and careful attention needs to be paid to this aspect of the context of each study in considering its findings.

| The purposes of scientific work

Only a few studies have probed students' ideas about the purpose of science. We focus here upon three studies which cover both 'real science' and 'school science' contexts and which employ quite different methodologies. Two involved a classroom investigation aimed at developing students' views of the nature of science; in the process, they obtained some information on how students see the purpose of scientific work. The third study was a large national survey.

Carey and her co-workers (1989) reported the effects of a specially designed three-week teaching programme on 12-year-old students' ideas about the nature and purposes of science. The teaching programme (which involved simple ideas about yeast) was designed to help children move from an inductive epistemology (where scientific knowledge is seen as 'emerging' from observation and hence providing a faithful representation of the world) to a hypothetico-deductive (or, in Carey and co-workers' terms, *constructivist*) epistemology (where observation and experimentation are seen as being purposeful, theory-driven activities). During the lessons, students were encouraged to reflect on various aspects of the nature of science; interviews were used to probe their views before and after teaching. The assumption underlying the approach taken by Carey and her team was that in order to gain an understanding of the constructed nature of scientific knowledge, and the inquiry process that yields this knowledge, students must be actively involved in proposing and evaluating their own explanations of natural phenomena, and be engaged in personal reflection on this process.

Seventy-six students from one year group in one school took part in the study. Carey *et al.* reported a range of student ideas, before the teaching programme, about the purpose of scientific work. These ranged from the view that science is about inventing cures and devices to views of science as seeking to develop a mechanistic understanding of the world (such as a scientific activity to find out *how* animals get oxygen). After teaching, they reported that some children presented slightly more sophisticated ideas. A few had even moved to a view of the purpose of science as developing explanations of natural phenomena (such as explaining *why* animals need to get oxygen).

Solomon *et al.* (1994) took a similar approach to Carey and co-workers in basing their research around a specially designed teaching intervention aimed at developing students' views of the nature of science. Their intervention extended over a twelve-month period and was based on episodes from the history of science. Students aged 11–14 years in five school classes (the total number involved is not reported, but is likely to be around seventy-five), were asked to complete a short questionnaire before and after teaching, and were then interviewed about their responses. The questions used a multiple-choice format, with the responses offered based on the range of positions expected by the reseachers. One item to probe students' ideas about the purposes of science asked: 'Why do you think that scientists do experiments?' The students selected one of three responses: to make new discoveries; to try out their explanations for why things happen; to make something which will help people.

Solomon *et al.* report that a relatively small number of students answered in terms of scientists 'making something to help people' and that this number further decreased after teaching. No 14-year-old student selected this response before or after teaching, though about 10 per cent of 11- to 13-year-olds did so before teaching. Before teaching they report 'worryingly little' evidence from interviews that students saw the 'explanation' of phenomena as a reason for scientists' work, although in responses to the questionnaire, 'explanation' obtained a more substantial showing, with about 40 per cent of students across the age range choosing this option. Between 50 and 60 per cent of all pupils opted for the 'discovery' response prior to teaching. The most striking effect of teaching on students' responses was to increase the numbers of students opting for the 'explanation' response, with 60–70 per cent of students now making this selection.

One methodological issue which arises from this study concerns the approach of asking students to select from three possible responses. Even though questionnaire responses were followed up in interviews, students' initial choice of response is constrained by the three options offered, none of which may capture precisely a student's view. The multiple-choice approach also relies heavily on students' interpretation of the wording of the question matching that intended by the researchers who framed the responses offered. It also obscures any variation of view within each answer category – though interviewing may go some way to addressing this. As regards the specific options offered to this questionnaire item, distinguishing between responses relating to 'discoveries' and those relating to 'helping people' might be rather difficult in practice (how would students express the view that 'discoveries are made to help people'). In a similar way, it is conceivable that a 'new discovery' might be thought of in terms of 'discovering an explanation for something'.

A further point concerns the shift to responses involving 'explanations' after teaching: might this not simply be due to a particular emphasis (in Solomon and co-workers' study, on explanation) throughout the teaching? Carey and her team note and address precisely this question. They acknowledge that their post-test required students to repeat points made by the teacher during teaching. They also note, however, that epistemological views were expressed by students after teaching which were not introduced directly by the teaching programme, and see this as evidence that changes represented more than simple repetition of memorized information.

Aikenhead *et al.* (1987) investigated students' ideas about the purposes of science as part of a very large survey of the views of Canadian high-school graduates on science–technology–society issues. Ninety-nine per cent of students surveyed (*n*=10,800) were in the age range 17–22 years. The sample included both students who were, and were not, studying science. Data were collected by means of written instruments in which students were given statements to classify as 'Agree', 'Disagree' or 'Not Sure'; they were then asked to write a paragraph to justify their position on each statement. The statements themselves were derived from students' answers to more open-ended questions used in a pilot phase of the study. The main findings from the survey are reported in a series of papers (Aikenhead 1987; Fleming 1987; Ryan 1987). The Fleming and Aikenhead papers include information about students' views of the purpose of scientific work.

To probe ideas about what motivates individual scientists in their work, students were asked to select one of three positions on why individual Canadian scientists are involved in generating scientific knowledge: to earn a decent salary, to earn recognition from other scientists, or to satisfy their curiosity. As already explained, these positions had been offered by students in response to an open-ended question used in the pilot phase of the study. The responses were varied, with the largest number of students thinking that scientists were motivated by a desire to satisfy their own curiosity. A large number of students also said that scientists tackled these problems in order to make the world a better place to live in. Aikenhead, Fleming and Ryan suggest that students' responses show that they do not distinguish between different sorts of scientific and technological activity. This clearly raises an important methodological issue for research in this area. Science covers a tremendous range of activities (from routine laboratory testing to multi-million pound particle physics); technology (which students may not distinguish clearly from science) broadens the scope further. There is, therefore, a very wide range of contexts and examples which individuals may call to mind in responding to any question about the purpose of scientific work. So enquiries about the purpose of science beg the questions: 'what purpose?' and 'which science?'. (This issue also applies, of course, to the other two features of understanding of the nature of science discussed below.)

Aikenhead, Fleming and Ryan's findings also show that students tended to treat science and technology as a unified enterprise (which the authors term 'technoscience') and suggested that both have a place in improving the quality of life for Canadians. Socioscientific issues tended to be viewed by students as technical problems, and the purpose of scientific work was seen as solving these technical problems to improve the quality of life. For example, over 50 per cent of the students believed that scientists and engineers should take a leading role in making important socioscientific decisions on issues such as energy use, because of their greater knowledge. The students believed that the government should coordinate scientific and technical research, to ensure it serves the public interest.

Taken together, the findings from these three studies suggest that many young people have an inductive view of science, seeing scientists as making discoveries about the world through careful observation. Experiments are conducted to find out what happens, either in general or when specific factors are manipulated. Very few see science as centrally concerned with developing explanations. Science is commonly viewed in an instrumental way, as a means of improving the human condition, finding cures for diseases and inventing new devices. In general, there is a lack of differentiation between science and technology.

| The nature and status of scientific knowledge

We now turn to what many would consider lies at the heart of an understanding of the nature of science: students' ideas about the nature and status of scientific knowledge. Many studies have been carried out, with a particular emphasis on students' views about the nature of theory and its relationship to evidence. Most have addressed this relationship in the specific context of school science, with rather fewer focusing on the work of scientists.

The coordination of theory and evidence

Students' ability to coordinate theory and evidence appropriately has been a focus of lively debate in recent years. The debate centres upon the issue of whether the ability to coordinate theory with evidence can be considered a generally applicable, age-related skill, or whether it depends fundamentally upon the domain of application. Before embarking on a more detailed discussion of this work, it is important to note that the question which has been explored is the extent to which young people can coordinate theory and evidence appropriately. The extent to which they see this as central to the work of scientists has received less attention.

Kuhn *et al.* (1988) argue for a 'domain-general view' of the coordination of theory and evidence. They present a case for the existence of generally applicable thinking skills. They suggest that these thinking skills change with age and cite the following skills as being necessary to achieve an 'ideal' ability to coordinate theory and evidence:

- The ability to think about a theory, rather than only think with it.
- The ability to encode and represent the evidence to be evaluated as an entity distinct from representation of the theory.
- The ability to set aside acceptance or rejection of a theory in order to

assess what the evidence by itself would mean for the theory, were it the only basis for making a judgement.

Kuhn and her colleagues presented their research subjects with a causal explanation (which they subsequently termed a 'theory') and a series of pieces of data (evidence), some of which were in agreement with the explanation while others were not. The research probed the way in which subjects coordinated evidence with explanation, and the conclusions they drew from this. The success of subjects in correctly identifying evidence of covariance (where a factor does affect an outcome) and non-covariance (where a factor has no effect on the outcome) are explored, as is the influence of the subject's commitment to the explanation under discussion as actually valid. The study was conducted in several parts and involved several hundred subjects ranging from 10-year-olds to lay adults, as well as a group of philosophy graduate students, included as 'experts' in coordinating theory and evidence.

The 'theories' were selected so that the research subjects would be unlikely to have any strong prior commitments to them. One was about the type of food that may make people more likely to catch a cold, another about the effects of various physical characteristics (e.g. the smoothness) of tennis balls on a player's service. 'Theories' of this sort have been criticized by Carey et al. (1989) as being quite different from the theories that students meet in science. For example, in the tennis ball context, subjects are asked to examine two sets of data and to generate theories about the influence of ball smoothness on a player's serve. This exercise involves making hypotheses based on patterns in the given data; this is rather different from, for example, making and testing predictions about the behaviour of a gas using a theoretical model, the kinetic model of gases.

Kuhn et al. (1988) found that younger students (below age 12) had difficulties with all of the types of reasoning involved; performance improved somewhat with age. Many students (including adults) interpreted data sets in different ways in relation to theories they espoused and those they did not. Kuhn and her colleagues suggest that this shows an inability to distinguish clearly between the theory itself and instances or non-instances of that theory. They also noted instances of adjusting theories to fit the evidence and of denying the evidence where it failed to match the theory.

The interpretation of these findings as providing evidence for a domain-general view has been challenged by Samarapungavan (1992). In an ingeniously designed study, Samarapungavan investigated the ability of children (age 6–11 years) to use each of four criteria in theory-choice tasks: range of explanatory power; non ad-hocness of explanation; empirical consistency; and logical consistency. Children were given theory-choice tasks set in the contexts of ideas about the Earth in Space (an area in which children are likely to have prior conceptual knowledge) and colour changes when using indicators (an area where they are likely to have little prior conceptual knowledge). The children's own ideas about the solar system were elicited prior to testing, and were classified as 'geocentric' or 'heliocentric'. Theory-choice tasks were then presented which were in agreement with the child's existing theories or in contrast to them. In these tasks, the children were presented with simple data about a phenomenon related either to the appearance of the night sky, or to the behaviour of unfamiliar chemicals when mixed. They were then given two possible theories which might explain the data. The theories were constructed to differ only with respect to one of the four criteria listed above.

Samarapungavan reports that 85–90 per cent of children in this age range (with little age-related difference) were able to make and explain theory-choices in terms of the four stated criteria, and there was little difference in the results in the two contexts. She acknowledges, however, that there is a difference between being able to choose the better of two theories on the criteria above, and actually using these criteria in science learning. Even so, she argues that her findings do not support the claim of Kuhn *et al.* that general skills in the coordination of theory and evidence develop with age, and are weak in the 6–11 age range. Rather, Samara-pungavan suggests that change in reasoning is accounted for in terms of the child's developing understanding of *concepts* in distinct contexts – a perspective which we will refer to as a 'domain-specific view'.

Brewer and Samarapungavan (1991) further argue that although young children may be able to use epistemological criteria, such as logical con-sistency, in evaluating theories, they are not necessarily commited to the use of such criteria in the way that members of the scientific community are. This may account for the difference between what an individual *can do* in a theory-choice situation, as opposed to what they *actually do* in other contexts; students may be capable of applying criteria in theory-choice but may not see the need to do so, or regard this as important in scientific work.

The studies referred to above relate to the psychological issue of students' abilities to coordinate theory and evidence. However, it is clear from much research on students' ideas that learning science is not simply a matter of changing personal explanations in the face of anomalous data. Rowell and Dawson (1983), for example, note that empirical counter-examples tend to be dealt with by young people in a variety of ways, other than abandoning an accepted theory (they might, for example, deny the validity of the evi-dence). Students are aware of the limitations of their equipment and their own data-collection skills, so that this 'resistance to falsification' of personal theories may be quite rational. Chinn and Brewer (1993), in a recent re-view, consider seven ways in which individuals resolve problems presented by anomalous data: (a) ignoring the anomalous data, (b) rejecting the anomalous data, (c) excluding the data from the domain of the theory in question, (d) holding the data in abeyance, (e) reinterpreting the data while retaining the theory, (f) reinterpreting the data and making peripheral changes to the theory, (g) accepting the data and changing the theory in question or adopting an alternative theory. In the next section, we will review some studies which explored how young people coordinate theory and evidence in the context of their own empirical enquiries.

Theory and evidence in empirical enquiry

As part of the study by Carey *et al.* (1989), which we referred to earlier, 12-year-olds were asked to describe what was meant by experimentation. This information was sought both before and after a teaching intervention. Carey and her team found that many students did not see hypotheses as based on factual knowledge about phenomena and saw experimentation as a disembodied process, not guided by ideas, questions or assumptions. Other students saw crude links between experiments and ideas, saying that experiments test 'to see if something works'. More sophisticated responses made clear distinctions between ideas and activities, and a few responses referred to the way in which data from experiments interact with ideas. As a result of their enquiry, Carey and her colleagues proposed four broad 'bands' into which students' epistemologies could be grouped.

- *Level 0*: students have no appreciation of science as an information-seeking enterprise.
- *Level 1*: students are not able to differentiate between theories and the evidence that supports the theory. They interpret evidence as instances or non-instances of the theory.
- *Level 2*: students are able to distinguish a theory from the evidence that supports it. These students hold a correspondence view of theories, seeing them as a faithful copy of nature.
- *Level 3*: students are able to distinguish between theories and the evidence that supports them. In addition, they are able to understand the way in which theories act as a motivation for experimentation.

Most students were at Level 1 or Level 2 before the teaching programme, with modest improvements resulting from teaching.

Karmiloff-Smith and Inhelder (1974) investigated the views of children aged 4–10 of empirical enquiry by closely observing them as they carried out a task. The children were presented with the problem of balancing objects on a simple pivot, the objects varying in terms of the distribution of their mass relative to the geometric centre, and the visual cues given about the distribution of mass. Thus in some cases the object would be a uniform beam, in others a beam which had been biassed with loading at one end. They found that the younger children tended to use a trial-and-error approach, achieving success in the balancing task. The older children were more likely to approach the problem with a theory in mind (that objects should balance at their geometric centre), and proceeded to make fine adjustments about the centre. Where this strategy did not work, the children claimed the task was impossible. Karmiloff-Smith and Inhelder suggested that this illustrates that counter-examples are seen by younger children as anomalies, rather than as evidence relating to a theory of balance, whereas older children proceed in an implicitly hypothetico-deductive way. It should be noted, of course, that this study was an exploration of children's 'practices of enquiry' which may, or may not, be reflected in their explicit views about empirical enquiry. Other studies, however, in contexts closely related to school science, tend to corroborate this shift with age away from action-based views of empirical enquiry towards more theory-based ones (see, for example, Metz 1991; Schauble *et al.* 1991; Solomon *et al.* 1994).

The epistemology of scientific knowledge

Larochelle and Désautels (1991) interviewed twenty-five secondary students about the nature of scientific knowledge and about scientific observation and experimentation. They made the point, which we have already noted, that there is no reason to assume that students' characterizations of their own empirical enquiry are the same as their characterizations of what scientists do. Their analysis of the interview data suggested that secondary students have a mainly 'technico-empiricist' conception of the nature of scientific knowledge, with little opportunity for creativity on the part of scientists in the process of knowledge production. 'Scientists do not create the facts; they notice them and are guided by their indisputable recurrence and empirical evidence' (Larochelle and Désautels 1991: 385).

As part of a study referred to earlier, Aikenhead (1987) investigated the beliefs of Canadian high-school graduates (age 17–22 years) about the characteristics and limitations of scientific knowledge. He reported that some students were aware that scientific models have changed in history. Few students appeared to view scientific models as provisional, adopting instead a naive realist view rather similar to Carey's Level 2 students. Many, however, suggested that theories developed in current research may be rejected quite soon as new data emerge. Some saw knowledge as fixed and not open to change, though more accurate investigations could lead to new, 'correct' knowledge. Only a few students argued that it was the interpretation of data, rather than its quantity or quality, which changed.

Summary

From the perspective of our present study, the principal messages from studies of the sort reviewed above concern students' ideas about the nature (and origins) of explanations and the extent to which these are seen as 'emerging from', or closely tied to, the data which they explain. In order to entertain the notion that a theory is conjectural, and to see a role for experiment in providing raw data for theorizing or as a test of theory, a student must be able to consider explanation and evidence as two separate 'entities'. The studies discussed above suggest that, so long as 'theories' are clearly stated and understood and the nature of tasks clearly explained, some students from early adolescence onwards are able to consider the implications of particular data items for a given theory, the proportion increasing with age. There is, however, less agreement about the extent to which younger children are able to do this, though it has been noted that there is a difference between the *ability* of young people to perform this task in carefully controlled experimental conditions and what happens when they undertake empirical enquiry. Furthermore, there is evidence that an individual's understanding of the conceptual content of a theory will influence his or her ability to relate it to evidence.

There is also considerable evidence, from several studies of quite different sorts, that many students adopt a naive realist interpretation of scientific theories, seeing them as emerging from collected data and so providing a faithful account of nature. Younger students are likely to view experimentation as 'simple finding out'; older students are more likely to recognize the role of ideas in stimulating, directing and influencing the interpretation of experiments.

| Science as a social enterprise

Rather less work has been carried out and reported on students' understanding of the social relationships within science and between science and the wider society than on students' ideas about scientific knowledge. This may reflect the emphasis in the school curriculum on individual empirical investigation and the relative neglect of the social dimensions of science. In this section, we review the findings of two studies which report on students' views of science as a social enterprise. Other findings from both studies have been discussed in earlier sections.

The characteristics of scientists

Solomon *et al.* (1994) used questionnaire and interview data (collected before and after the teaching intervention) to describe the range of students' images of science and scientists (although they reported on students' images of scientists from the data collected prior to teaching only). Some students (aged 11–14 years) drew upon familiar images such as the 'cartoon scientist' (Mead and Metraux 1957; Chambers 1983), or science teachers and pupils in science lessons. Other images of scientists they reported were the vivisectionist, the technologist (who makes products to help people) and the entrepreneur (who seeks to make new discoveries first). This latter image attributes strongly competitive motives to scientists. Solomon and her colleagues noted that students seemed to hold a range of images of scientists simultaneously, and stated that a purpose of their teaching interventions was to broaden that range rather than to replace particular images. Drawing on the findings of the large-scale survey of Canadian students discussed above, Ryan (1987) reported students' views on the honesty and objectivity of scientists. A majority of students thought that scientists are trained to act in a logical, methodical, analytical, open-minded way and that these attitudes would transfer into their everyday lives.

When asked directly about the bias shown by scientists in their work compared to non-scientists, a range of views emerged. About a quarter of the students thought that nobody, scientists included, is free of bias. A slightly higher proportion thought that both scientists and non-scientists are unbiased in their work, with about a quarter of respondents arguing that it is more important for scientists to be unbiased than non-scientists. Some students suggested that individual scientists would differ in the extent to which bias affected their work. The majority of students thought that scientists were no more honest as individuals than non-scientists, but that honesty might be more important in their professional activities than for non-scientists. About a quarter of respondents thought that scientists as a group tend to be more honest than non-scientists.

The social nature of scientific communities

Reporting on the same survey of Canadian students, Aikenhead (1987) reported their views on the issue of whether social contact between scientists within a community would be beneficial to their work. The great majority of respondents said that social contact between scientists would improve the performance of individual scientists. Their view was justified by stating that the exchange of ideas between scientists would result in better informed research taking place, or the idea that a community environment is more productive for the scientist to think in and will aid progress. A small number of students suggested that scientists should be involved in social activity in order to gain insights into the society which their work is designed to improve! This view appears to follow from a perception of scientists as working in solitary isolation screened from contact with society.

The students were also asked about the reasons for disagreements between scientists on issues such as the safety of low-level background radiation. Their positions ranged from explanations in terms of lack of knowledge or inaccurate experimental work, to statements that personal values, opinions and interests would affect the conclusions drawn by scientists.

The relationship of scientific communities to other social groups

Again from the Canadian survey, Fleming (1987) reported students' reactions to contrasting statements on energy policy: that scientists and engineers should make decisions on energy policy because they know the facts best; or, alternatively, that scientists and engineers should be the last people to decide on such issues – because the decision affects everyone, the public should decide.

About half the students adopted a technocratic position, justifying their view by referring to the expertise of scientists or the lack of bias in scientific knowledge compared with the bias among other interest groups which might be involved in decision-making. Other students used arguments about democracy and democratic values to justify their position, or suggested that social problems cannot be solved with scientific knowledge and technological expertise alone.

The students were also asked to respond to statements claiming that science and technology either can, or cannot, offer help in resolving social problems such as poverty, crime, unemployment, overpopulation and the threat of nuclear war. The students' responses covered a range of positions. Some claimed that science and technology made some of the social problems worse, for example that computers cause unemployment. Others distinguished science and technology *per se* from the way in which they are used by individuals and groups in society. A small number of responses stated that the problems listed lie outside the domain of science, and that science and technology are therefore of no relevance to solving these problems. Some responses drew distinctions between particular problems listed, arguing that science had a bearing on some problems but not others.

Fleming also reported students' views about the social control of science. Many students suggested that research funding should only be agreed when scientists can show, in advance, what the return on the investment will be in terms of improved quality of life. Some students argued that, although science *should* improve the quality of life, it is not always possible to predict this in advance. A small number of students stated that science should be funded because of its aim of developing explanations and understanding rather than of improving the quality of life. When asked directly if research should be funded for the sake of generating new knowledge alone, most students answered affirmatively, but justified their position by saying that increased knowledge would lead to improvements in the quality of life.

A range of views was also expressed about the role of government in determining what topics scientists should research. Some students argued that scientists should have a free choice of research topic, as they are the group best able to identify problems and also to identify how the quality of life might be improved. Some students, on the other hand, suggested that those who hold the purse strings have a right to determine what research is undertaken. Others expressed compromise viewpoints, stating that scientists and governments should cooperate in deciding what is to be researched.

Summary

The fact that the discussion above is based heavily on one single large survey is, itself, an indication of the lack of systematic research in this area. The main findings are that young people draw upon a range of social images of science and scientists. A very common image is of the scientist as someone who works to produce artifacts (or, occasionally, knowledge) which will be of benefit to humankind. Scientists, because of their expertise and knowledge, are seen as being in a good position to offer (or to search for) solutions to practical problems.

| Reflections on research methodology

One purpose of the review of research presented in this chapter has been to identify key findings and to establish the extent of consensus in the findings of studies of different sorts. This we have done in the course of the discussion above. Research studies also raise methodological issues. Again some of these have been identified and explored. Here we will draw together these methodological issues, identifying key similarities and differences in the studies discussed.

A first, and quite critical, issue is whether questions and probes are set in specific contexts or asked generally, and in a decontextualized setting. An example of the former is Aikenhead and co-workers' exploration of students' views about the role of science in solving social problems, in which they use specific contexts like energy generation or nuclear power; examples of the latter are direct open questions like 'What is an hypothesis?', used by Carey *et al.* (1989). Both approaches have problems. The decontextualized approach has the difficulty that it is impossible to know what students have in mind in giving a response. Their answers may be based on specific examples they have in mind, but which are undeclared. Similarly, in interpreting students' responses to Solomon and co-workers' question, 'Why do you think that scientists do experiments?', it may be crucial to know what kind of 'scientist' the student has in mind, and what sort of 'experiment'. Some would see this uncertainty as completely undermining the data obtained by methods of this sort. Setting questions in specific contexts avoids this weakness, but makes it more difficult to generalize from the responses obtained; perhaps these are specific to the contexts chosen.

A second and related issue is that, when questions are asked outside any framing context, the researcher obtains information about students' *espoused* views. These may or may not be the same as the views they express implicitly in action. At the opposite extreme, information might be collected about students' *implicit* views by making inferences from their actions as they undertake specific tasks. For example, Karmiloff-Smith and Inhelder (1974) probed students' views of empirical enquiry by involving them directly in practical balancing tasks (which is quite different from asking them about the nature of empirical enquiry in a decontextualized way). This distinction between espoused views and views implicit in action is an important one. Rowell and Dawson (1983), for example, have shown that students' views of the nature of science may not be reflected in the way that they approach scientific investigations. Students assert one thing and do something quite different!

If questions and tasks are set in context, a further issue which arises is choice of 'real science' or 'school science' as the context. So, for example, Aikenhead *et al.* (1987) probed students' views of the work of scientists, whereas the studies by Carey *et al.* (1989) and Solomon *et al.* (1994) were set in classroom contexts and so were more likely to evoke ideas and images from that context. There is, as we have indicated above, a critical issue about the extent and nature of the 'knowledge' on which students can draw in answering questions about 'real science' in particular.

Finally, research approaches differ in the way in which data are treated. One approach is to use a normative (or 'nomothetic') approach. Aspects of the nature of science which are of interest are first identified; the content of those aspects are then specified and used as a basis for evaluating students' ideas. A research question might focus, for example, on the nature of scientific enquiry and responses would be analysed to see the extent to which students' ideas matched a particular pre-specified view (for instance, the hypothetico-deductive view). An alternative approach is to seek to elicit and to describe the views that students hold, attempting to make sense of them from within the students' perspective. This is an 'ideographic' approach in which the researcher seeks to understand students' responses in their own terms, rather than simply to judge their level of compatibility with a pre-specified norm. Of the research described in this chapter, the multiple-choice options offered by Solomon *et al.* (1994) could be seen as embodying normative assumptions. So, too, does the view underpinning Carey and co-workers' (1989) study that a hypothetico-deductive view is more sophisticated than an inductive one, if this is seen as a general conclusion rather than in relation to the specific piece of teaching they use. On the other hand, Carey *et al.* develop their four-band taxonomy of students' views of experimentation ideographically, basing it upon students' responses to interview questions.

These issues, relating to research methodology, will be considered again in Chapter 5, where we describe and discuss the design of our own study.

5 | Investigating students' ideas about the nature of science

In Chapters 2–4, we reviewed three different strands of background literature which we have drawn upon in framing our study of students' views and representations of the nature of science. Chapter 2 reviews the position papers – writings which argue for the importance of an understanding of the nature of science to particular groups and for particular purposes and reasons. Chapter 3 is an overview of the literature on the nature of science; it explores key issues and distinctions which need to be taken into account in framing an empirical study and in interpreting its outcomes. In Chapter 4, we discuss some important recent studies of students' ideas about aspects of the nature of science. Through these chapters we have identified three features of an understanding of the nature of science which provide a focus for a study of students' representations. These features are an understanding of: *the purposes of scientific work; the nature and status of scientific knowledge*; and *science as a social enterprise.*

In this chapter, we identify specific questions of interest about students' thinking in each of these three areas. We then describe briefly the research tasks (or *probes*) which we developed and used to explore students' representations and explain the reasons for some of the decisions which underpin our choice of research strategy and methods. Finally, we explain how these probes were administered and outline the methods of analysis which we employed.

| Research questions

In designing a study of students' representations, the step from general features of interest to specific questions which can guide the development of research tools is an important one. All three features are rich and complex and there are many facets of students' views about them which could be explored. The questions which we chose to frame the study were selected in an attempt to map what we considered to be important aspects of students' ideas about the nature of science, bearing in mind the literatures presented in Chapters 3 and 4. The questions act as signposts to indicate those aspects of students' representations of the nature of science which we are interested in portraying. The questions chosen, which are presented and discussed below, are also listed in Table 5.1, where they are numbered for ease of reference.

Table 5.1 The research questions which framed this enquiry into students' representations of the nature of science.

The purposes of scientific work
1.1 What do students see as characterizing the kinds of questions which scientists address?

The nature and status of scientific knowledge

About experimentation
2.1 What do students see as being the purpose of experimentation? What do they see as characterizing the process of experimentation?

About the nature of explanation in science
2.2 What do students consider the status of scientific theories to be? How do they consider theories relate to phenomena? To what extent do they see theories and laws as conjectural?
2.3 What types of warrants (if any) are drawn upon by students to justify their acceptance or rejection of theories?

About the evaluation of theories
2.4 How do students think that theories are evaluated? Do they consider theories separately from the phenomena which they explain?
2.5 Can students evaluate theories appropriately using empirical evidence? Are they able to evaluate theories independently of their belief in the theory?

Science as a social enterprise
3.1 Do students see the scientific enterprise as a social (as opposed to an individual) endeavour?
3.2 How do students interpret conflicts in ideas within the scientific community? How do they see these being resolved?
3.3 What do students see as the influence of society at large on the generation of scientific knowledge and on the application of that knowledge in specific contexts?

The purposes of scientific work

Here we are interested in students' perceptions of the purposes of scientific work. We wish to portray the kinds of questions which students think are of interest to scientists, their ideas about what science seeks to provide (or produce) and about the boundaries of its interests. The following question was used to frame our enquiry into students' representations of this feature:

> What do students see as characterizing the kinds of questions which scientists address?

The nature and status of scientific knowledge

This feature is a large and complex one with a number of strands. The first concerns the procedures of empirical enquiry through which scientific knowledge has been, and continues to be, obtained. We see empirical enquiry as involving the collection and use of data. Such data may provide the accounts of phenomena which require explanation or may be used to test proposed explanations (for example, through experimentation).

Although we do not see empirical enquiry in science as being limited to experimentation, in the sense of a deliberate intervention to produce observational data, we recognize that the term 'experiment' is widespread in students' own talk about science learning and in classroom discourse. Given this, it therefore seemed important to explore the meanings attributed to it and the purposes experiments were seen to serve. The questions which framed our enquiry were:

> What do students see as being the purpose of experimentation?
>
> What do students see as characterizing the process of experimentation?

A second strand within this feature concerns the nature of explanation in science. Our questions were framed to portray two aspects of students' representations, the first relating to the status of scientific theories and the second to students' warrants for accepting or rejecting theories:

> What do students consider the status of scientific theories to be? How do they consider theories relate to phenomena? To what extent do they see theories and laws as conjectural?
>
> What types of warrants (if any) are drawn upon by students to justify their acceptance or rejection of theories?

A third strand, about the evaluation of theories, attempts to portray the ways in which students see theory as being related to evidence. The questions were:

> How do students think that theories are evaluated? Do they consider theories separately from the phenomena which they explain?
>
> Can students evaluate theories appropriately using empirical evidence? Are they able to evaluate theories independently of their belief in the theory?

Science as a social enterprise

Again, in this area there is a very wide range of issues which might be addressed. Students' views of science as a social enterprise include their ideas about both the internal workings and the external relations of the scientific community. Do students, for instance, see scientists as individuals working in isolation from other scientists, or as members of teams and networks? If scientists are thought to work in extended communities, then under what circumstances might scientific disputes arise and how might such disputes be resolved? How does scientific research relate to wider social issues and concerns? Are scientists the best placed people to offer advice on socioscientific issues such as a national energy policy? The specific questions which framed our inquiry were:

> Do students see the scientific enterprise as a social (as opposed to an individual) endeavour?
>
> How do students interpret conflicts in ideas within the scientific community? How do they see these being resolved?
>
> What do students see as the influence of society at large on the generation of scientific knowledge and on the application of that knowledge in specific contexts?

We will now describe briefly the instruments (or probes) which we developed to explore these questions with school students.

| The research probes

Six research probes were developed through a process of small-scale trials. Essentially, these probes provide both stimulus material and associated tasks which prepare the ground for a semi-structured interview. They orient students to the topic of research interest, stimulate them to think about specific issues and questions in given contexts and provide opportunities for reflection. At an early stage we decided to set all probes in specific science contexts rather than to ask general questions about science and scientists. The issues at stake here have already been rehearsed in previous chapters and are considered again at greater length later in this chapter. Our view was that the problems of interpreting responses to general questions were so great as to undermine the data. Students' answers and views would be based, inevitably, on specific instances and examples which they called to mind; without knowledge of these, interpretation would be difficult and perhaps impossible. We decided therefore that it was essential to set questions in specific contexts and to anchor interviews and follow-up questions clearly to specific situations. All probes used more than one context, so that strongly context-specific features of responses might be detected.

The study was designed in such a way that most of the research questions were addressed by more than one probe, every question was addressed in more than one context and all three features of understanding of the nature of science were covered. Several were set in school science contexts, while others drew on contexts from both school science and 'real' science. One, exploring students' understanding of science as a social enterprise, was set wholly in the content of the work of professional scientists. Each of the six probes is reviewed briefly below to give readers an overview of the range and focus of the research tools which were used. Specific details of the probes will be given together with the descriptions and analysis of students' responses in Chapters 6–9.

Scientific Questions

The students were presented with a range of questions. They were asked to classify each question as to whether or not it was a 'scientific question' (a question that scientists would be interested to find out more about), giving their reasons.

From the students' responses we hoped to gain insights into:

- students' ideas about the features which characterize questions as 'scientific' and 'not scientific' (research question 1.1);
- the perceived limits of the range of questions which can be addressed from a scientific perspective (research question 1.1);
- the ideas which students have about the role of experimentation and empirical evidence generally in evaluating scientific knowledge claims (research questions 2.1 and 2.4).

Experiment

The students were presented with a number of cards describing particular activities taken from school science, real science and everyday contexts. They were asked to classify each activity as 'an experiment' or 'not an experiment' or 'not sure', giving reasons. They were then asked to explain and justify their overall classification of the set of activities. Follow-up questions explored the perceived relationship between theory and evidence in the contexts provided.

From the students' responses we hoped to gain insights into:

- students' ideas about the purpose of experimentation (research question 2.1);
- the criteria used by students to characterize experiments and experimentation (research question 2.1);
- the ideas which students have about the role of experimentation and empirical evidence generally in evaluating scientific knowledge claims (research question 2.4).

Theory Stories

This probe sought to provide a context for subjects to talk about theories. A number of short stories were written, each involving children talking about a 'theory' and the evidence that might support it. In the final version of the probe, three stories were presented to the students. The stories dealt with the rusting of iron, the behaviour of air on heating and the germ theory of decay. For each, the students were asked to explain what they understood by the word 'theory' and how each theory could be tested.

From the students' responses we hoped to gain insights into:

- students' ideas about the status of theories and about their relationship to phenomena (research question 2.2);
- the extent to which students see theories as conjectural (research question 2.2);
- whether students consider that theories can be evaluated using empirical evidence (research question 2.4);
- whether students consider theories separately from the phenomena which they explain (research question 2.4).

Warrants for Belief

The students were presented with a familiar theoretical proposition, asked whether they had heard of it before, and whether or not they believed it. If so, they were then asked to give their reasons for believing the theory to be true. The two propositions used related to the ideas 'the Earth is round like a ball' and 'an electric current flows round a simple circuit when it is switched on'.

From the students' responses we hoped to gain insights into:

- the extent to which students see theories as conjectural (research question 2.2);
- the types of warrants which are drawn upon by students to justify their acceptance or rejection of a theory (research question 2.3).

Theory and Evidence

The students were presented with several possible explanations for a set of phenomena related to two contexts: simple electric circuits, and floating and sinking. They were asked to choose the explanation they felt was best. (In the 'Electric circuits' context, the students were first shown some simple demonstrations to remind them of some key facts to take into account in choosing an explanation; this was not felt to be necessary for the 'Floating and sinking' context.) In the 'Electric circuits' context, the students were then asked to use their chosen explanation to make predictions about a series of new situations; the actual behaviour was then demonstrated and the students were asked to consider whether this behaviour supported the chosen theory or not, and to justify their decisions. In the 'Floating and sinking' context, the students were simply asked whether each of a series of specific examples of floating and sinking objects were consistent or not with their explanation. In both contexts, the students' reasoning was probed.

From the students' responses we hoped to gain insights into:

- the role which students see for empirical evidence in evaluating a theory or explanation (research question 2.5);
- whether students' evaluation of theories is related to their personal acceptance or rejection of the theory (research question 2.5);
- whether students can consider theories separately from the phenomena which they explain and can evaluate theories using empirical evidence (research questions 2.4 and 2.5).

Closure of Debates

In a whole-class setting, the students were given background information about a controversial issue involving science, using a specially prepared booklet and an audiotape presentation. Two issues were used: the dispute surrounding Wegener's theory of continental drift in the 1920s and the current debate about irradiation of food. After presentation of one of the issues (lasting about 20 minutes), the groups of students were asked to discuss some key questions about the reasons for expert disagreement, and about what might lead (or had led) to its resolution – the closure of the debate. The groups were then interviewed by a researcher about their views on these questions.

From the students' responses we hoped to gain insights into:

- the extent to which students see the scientific enterprise as a social (as opposed to an individual) endeavour (research question 3.1);
- the ways in which students interpret the emergence and resolution of conflicts in the scientific community (research question 3.2);
- the ways in which students interpret the influence of society at large on the generation of scientific knowledge and the application of this knowledge in actual contexts (research question 3.3).

The probes are described in more detail in Chapters 6, 7 and 9, where the students' responses to the probes are discussed.

Designing the study: methodological issues and decisions

In choosing an interview study, with each interview stimulated and focused by a specific task, we were opting for a middle path between the use of a written survey instrument and a more naturalistic observation study. Our reason for rejecting the survey approach centred on the nature of the issues we wished to explore and the data we wished to collect. Ideas about the nature of science are subtle and complex and it is often difficult to find the most appropriate language in framing a question and, for the respondent, in providing an answer. We are not confident that survey questions with multiple-choice or open responses can be written in such a way as to overcome these difficulties. It cannot be assumed that the question will be understood, and responded to, with the meaning the questioner intended. Responses to open items are likely to raise further questions of clarification or elaboration; multiple-choice items constrain students' responses into pre-determined channels and, by forcing a decision, may misrepresent the frequency of certain views. In any event, the development of a survey instrument would require an initial more exploratory study to determine the key questions, to resolve issues of phrasing and intelligibility and, if multiple-choice responses were used, to indicate the range of options which should be offered and the terms in which they should be expressed.

At the opposite end of the methodological spectrum would be a study based on observing students in situations where their understanding of the nature of science might become apparent. A possible location for this would be the school science classroom. So one might, for instance, observe children in normal science classes and ask them about what they thought they were doing and why. Only some class activities, however, would raise issues of interest, and even coverage of the range of issues and questions of interest would be difficult to achieve. Also, variations of context and setting would be considerable, the researcher imposing almost no constraints on the situations observed. There is also a further limitation to such an approach, in that activities conducted in science lessons may provide little potential for addressing the work of practising scientists; school science is conducted for different purposes than 'real' science and students may recognize this.

While we recognized that such a naturalistic approach would provide important information about the way science is portrayed and communicated in classrooms, we were concerned that, in an initial enquiry into school students' representations, it would be helpful to have some consistency in the tasks set for the students. We therefore decided to use an interview approach, based around a series of probes, as the best means of enabling us to focus students on issues and questions of interest, while allowing for clarification and in-depth probing of responses as required.

Several important issues were also raised by the format of the interview probes themselves. The design of these probes, which presented issues and asked questions in specific contexts, reflected our primary aim of eliciting students' ideas about the nature of science in their own terms. We wanted to understand these views, from the student's perspective, rather than to compare them with the 'correct response'. We have indicated, in Chapter 3, the problems we see in claiming that certain understandings of the nature of science are 'better' in general; their merits must be judged in specific situations. Hence it is essential that we know what contexts the student is considering in making more general and abstract statements about science or scientific knowledge. So the study was framed in 'ideographic' terms, rather than 'nomothetic' ones. This ideographic emphasis was also reflected in the design of the specific probes.

As we mentioned earlier, we chose not to ask decontextualized questions (such as 'what is an experiment?'). Such questions may enable probing of students' espoused views, but they result in serious problems of interpretation of students' responses. In the example above, for instance, the word 'experiment' may be used with a variety of different meanings in mind. Scientists do, after all, perform experiments for a range of different reasons, and there are legitimate 'alternative' meanings for 'experiment' in everyday discourse. The student, therefore, faces a problem if asked to respond to a question without any framing context, and the researcher faces an equal problem in trying to make sense of that response without a context to locate it in.

In contrast to this, our probes began from specific examples or contexts. The initial questions were about a single context; the follow-up questions raised more abstract issues, but still in relation to the context under discussion. Subsequent questions may have asked students to consider common features of their answers in the different contexts used in the probe, pushing them towards more general, abstract ideas, but still retaining a link with a given set of contexts. Conclusions about students' representations of entities such as theories, and activities such as experimentation, can then be based on responses to a series of contexts, and nuances of meaning can be explored.

Deciding to set all probes in context, of course, raises other issues. One concerns the choice of contexts. Here a key issue is the balance between school science and real science contexts. We cannot assume that students' views about the *nature of science* are the same as their views of the *nature of school science*! Indeed, differences in these views might be seen as appropriate. Also, students' ideas about school science are likely to be based on more direct and more extensive experience than their ideas about real science. These considerations reinforce our view that it is essential for the context of any question or interview discussion to be made as clear and explicit as possible.

One final point needs to be made about the kinds of contexts and examples we used in some probes. Where probes involved theories or explanations, we selected examples which had a significant conceptual content, unlike, for example, the rather artificial empirical correlations used by Kuhn *et al.* (1988) as 'theories'. We were interested in the ways in which students relate theories to phenomena in contexts similar to those that feature in the school science curriculum. Students are likely to have expectations, and possibly explanations, about such phenomena. It is students' reasoning about such contexts and such forms of explanation which are of interest. This meant, of course, that contexts had to be selected so that their conceptual content was familiar and accessible (to some extent) to students across the 9–16 age range. Part of the function of the probes was to allow the students a little time to familiarize themselves with the context and the conceptual understanding involved before addressing any of the more subtle metacognitive issues about the nature of science.

The study was a cross-age survey. In part, this decision related to the timing and context of the research, begun at a time when the then current National Curriculum for England and Wales contained an explicit Attainment Target on *The Nature of Science*. This had to be constructed without the benefit of a research base of information on students' likely understandings, or of pathways along which these might develop. It seemed important to explore students' ideas in order to inform subsequent developments of this curriculum aspect. (In the event, changes were made to the National Curriculum before the research was completed.) A cross-age study is attractive because it allows data to be collected from students with very different amounts of experience of school science and is likely, therefore, to provide a wide range of ideas and views, of varying sophistication. A further attraction was that it might allow us to explore issues raised by other researchers about the nature and extent of changes with age of students' reasoning about some of these matters. A cross-age study might enable us to characterize the reasoning of populations of students at different ages, and to search for any similarities, differences and possible trends within and between age groups. It did not, of course, allow us to draw conclusions about pathways of development of understanding of individual students.

| Development and administration of the probes

A trial version of each probe was first used with a small sample of students aged 9 and 16 (*n*=4–6 at each age). In these trials, we noted that pairs of students tended initially to discuss the conceptual content of particular contexts, and were therefore much better placed to address the associated metacognitive issues, than students working by themselves. In the main study, interviews were therefore carried out with pairs of students for all probes (apart from **Closure of Debates**, where the students worked in groups of four) and student discussion time was allowed for. Also, during each trial the opportunity was taken to try out a range of possible contexts for each probe. **Theory and Evidence**, for example, was piloted in a wide range of contexts, 'electrical circuits' and 'floating and sinking' being chosen for the main study.

In administering the probes, care was taken to ensure that the students were not exposed to the same context in two different probes (the phenomenon of a balloon expanding when heated is, for example, used in both **Experiment** and **Theory Stories**). In order to avoid this sort of overlap, the probes were used in the following combinations:

- **Experiment** and **Warrants for Belief**
- **Theory Stories**
- **Scientific Questions** and **Theory and Evidence**

No single student was interviewed about more than two probes and the total interview time was between 20 and 40 minutes. The interviews were conducted in schools. They were held in a quiet room away from normal lessons and were administered in a calm, friendly and informal atmosphere. At the start of the interview, the students were told that we needed their help in trying to find out how pupils think about science and that they would be asked to talk and think about two questions. All the interviews were conducted by one of two trained interviewers and each interview was audiotaped in full.

Administration of the **Closure of Debates** probe was rather different from the others. In this case, the probe was administered to whole classes of 16-year-olds working in groups of four. This format was used in order that the students could be introduced to the necessary background to a particular issue (either continental drift or food irradiation), before carrying out activities which would allow us to explore ideas about how such debates are resolved within the scientific community. The **Closure of Debates** probe was trialled at ages 12 and 16 years and it was found that the level of background knowledge required was too great for the 12-year-old students. As a result, this probe was administered to the 16-year-olds only in the main study. As six groups within each class had to be interviewed at the same time, as soon as possible after completing the group discussion task, a team of researchers took part in data collection. For practical reasons, therefore, the sample size for **Closure of Debates** was smaller than for the other probes.

Details of the sample

Approximately thirty pairs of students were interviewed at each of the three age points (9, 12 and 16 years) for each probe (except for **Closure of Debates**). These ages were chosen to give as large a range as possible

Table 5.2 Number of pairs (or groups) of students responding to each probe.

Probe	Number of pairs		
	9 years	12 years	16 years
Scientific Questions	31	26	32
Experiment	31	32	33
Theory Stories	31	28	32
Warrants for Belief	28	32	33
Theory and Evidence	26	36	33
Closure of Debates	Number of groups of four		
Food irradiation	—	—	13
Continental drift	—	—	13

across the years of compulsory schooling, while also ensuring that the probes were accessible, at some level, to all the students involved. For this reason, the lower age limit was set at 9 years. The students attended six primary schools (5–11 years), two middle schools (8–13 years) and seven high schools (11–16 or 18 years) in one local education authority in the North of England. The schools were chosen from a wide range of city, suburban and semi-rural settings, drawing students from a mix of low- and middle-income catchment areas.

Pairs of students of the same sex were selected by their class teachers (primary and middle) or science teachers (secondary) from the top, middle and bottom of the ability range within each school to provide a sample at each age which was representative of the full ability range. The teachers were also asked to select pupils who would be prepared to talk with each other and with an interviewer. There is no reason to suppose that these students' experience of school science, or their exposure to implicit or explicit views on the nature of science, is other than typical of students of this age in the UK more generally.

Table 5.2 provides details of the sample size for each probe at each age.

| Analysis of data

Audiotapes for each of the interviews were transcribed in full and the transcripts were used as the basis of subsequent analysis. For all probes, an initial analysis was carried out ideographically, using coding categories derived from students' responses. This involved coding both decisions and the reasons or justifications for these decisions. For several probes, a second stage of analysis involved looking for patterns in responses to the different contexts, or examples, used in the probe. In the case of **Theory and Evidence**, the complexity of the task, coupled with the variation in students' responses, meant that a further level of analysis, based on expected patterns of reasoning, was also used. The analysis of students' responses is explained and discussed in much greater detail in Chapters 6–9, where students' responses to each probe are presented and patterns of response are identified. Chapter 6 examines students' ideas about the purposes of scientific work, drawing on the **Scientific Questions** probe. Chapter 7 then examines students' ideas about the nature and status of scientific knowledge, drawing on the **Experiment, Theory Stories, Theory and Evidence** and **Warrants for Belief** probes. Chapter 8 involves a further, and different, level of analysis in which we try to draw together evidence from all probes used across the 9–16 age range to present a general typology of students' representations of the three features of understanding of the nature of science. Finally, in Chapter 9, we examine 16-year-old students' ideas about science as a social enterprise, drawing principally on the **Closure of Debates** probe.

6 | Students' characterizations of the purposes of scientific work

In this chapter, we report on students' views about what characterizes scientific work and what they see as distinguishing it from other human pursuits. It is important to bear in mind, as discussed in Chapter 4, that scientific work is carried out for a variety of purposes in a range of institutional settings. Some scientists work in laboratories undertaking routine monitoring or screening tasks; others work in interdisciplinary teams on specific problems of design or manufacture in industry. It is the minority who work at the frontiers of current scientific knowledge in fields such as astronomy, particle physics or neurophysiology, and even here most are engaged in 'normal science' rather than in challenging fundamental theoretical structures.

As we indicated in Chapter 3, it is also difficult to draw clear distinctions between science and other ways of knowing; for example, there is no clear consensus about the boundary between the natural and the social sciences. Even viewing science as being characterized by its methods is problematic. In some domains, it is possible, for example, to test knowledge claims through experiments or planned interventions; in others, such as geology or evolutionary biology, such interventions are impossible and it is necessary to rely on the systematic collection and coordination of evidence.

In our study, we were interested in finding out what young people see as the purposes of scientific work. The specific question which we asked was:

> What do students see as characterizing the kinds of questions which scientists address?

Bearing in mind the diversity of scientific activity, it is unlikely that young people will have coherent generalized views about the purposes of science. It is more likely that they will draw on a range of characterizations in different contexts, and these may or may not have common features. For this reason, among others, it was important to probe students' views in a wide range of contexts. This was done in the **Scientific Questions** probe.

| The Scientific Questions probe

The probe consisted of a set of eleven questions (See Table 6.1). These questions were chosen to span natural and social phenomena, 'school science' as well as 'real science' activities, and to include some questions which are amenable to empirical testing and some which, for various reasons, are not.

Table 6.1 Questions used in the **Scientific Questions** probe.

Question	Basis of judgement	Commentary
Which kind of fabric is waterproof?	Empirical evidence	Natural phenomenon; familiar school science activity
*Which is the best programme on TV?	Aesthetic judgement	Social phenomenon
*Is it wrong to keep dolphins in captivity?	Ethical values	Natural phenomenon
How do birds find their way over long distances?	Empirical evidence	Natural phenomenon
*What diet is best to keep babies healthy?	Empirical evidence	Natural phenomenon
*Is it cheaper to buy a large or a small packet of washing powder?	Economics and personal evaluation of quality	Social phenomenon
*How was the Earth made?	Empirical evidence	Natural phenomenon; value issues (possibly religious commitments) involved
*Is the Earth's atmosphere heating up?	Empirical evidence	Natural phenomenon
Do ghosts haunt old houses at night?	Empirical evidence	Natural phenomenon; existence contested
What kind of bacteria are in the water supply?	Empirical evidence	Natural phenomenon
Can any metal be made into a magnet?	Empirical evidence	Natural phenomenon; familiar school science activity

*Questions analysed in more detail.

Administration of the probe

The questions were presented one by one, on cards, to pairs of students. The students were asked to consider the questions and to state whether each was a scientific question, not a scientific question or whether they were not sure, and to give the reason for their decision. They were told that scientific questions are questions that scientists might want to find out more about. The pairs were given time to classify all the questions and to justify their choices, without further probing by the interviewer. After they had completed this, the interviewer talked with them about their choices. In order to see whether the students had any general representation of the characteristics of science, the interview ended with the students being asked: 'In general, what makes a question a scientific question?'

| Results

Features mentioned in characterizing scientific questions

A striking feature of students' responses to the **Scientific Questions** probe was the range of views offered and the diversity of features drawn upon to justify those viewpoints. It was therefore necessary, after transcribing the responses, to produce an analysis scheme which reflected this diversity while identifying common features across contexts. First, the students' classification of each question (as a scientific question, not a scientific question or not sure) was noted. In practice, a variety of justifications for these classifications was made by the students, and the next stage of analysis involved grouping similar justifications offered for particular questions. Finally, the groupings across questions were reviewed and a common coding scheme for the justifications for all the questions was produced.

The students' justifications for classifying the questions as scientific or not tended to focus upon three features:

- Whether the question was open to empirical investigation; that is, investigation involving the collection of data, either measurements or observations.
- The nature of the domain of the question; whether it was considered to address natural phenomena or not.
- The perceived personal and institutional characteristics of scientific work and how these were thought to relate to the question.

Different types of responses relating to each of these three features were identified and a classification scheme of response types for each feature was devised. The students' answers and justifications were then classified using this scheme of response codes. In their discussion, the students often referred to more than one feature in justifying their decision. In such cases, the type of response given for each feature was coded, resulting in multiple codes being given to students' responses where appropriate. For example, discussions which mentioned both empirical testing and the domain of the question were classified with codes on each of these two features. Furthermore, in cases where pairs of students disagreed, or where different arguments were put forward by each member of a pair, each type of response was coded, again resulting in multiple codes. Each occasion when a code was given was called a 'coding decision'. In order to show the profile of representations at each age for each question and to consider age-related trends, the number of coding decisions for each particular type of response was totalled for each age group and calculated as a percentage of the total number of coding decisions for that age group.

We were interested to discover whether there were any age-related trends in the types of justifications which students gave for judging a question to be scientific or not. In order to do this, the number of student responses which referred to each of the three types of justification (empirical investigability, the domain of the question and the perceived personal and institutional characteristics of scientists) was totalled across six of the questions (those marked with an asterisk in Table 6.1). These six questions were chosen so as to include a balance of questions for which different types of justification were appropriate.

Empirical investigability

The students commonly suggested that, for a question to be regarded as scientific, it should be amenable to some sort of empirical investigation. In responding to the task, the students elaborated on what they meant by this and a number of distinct representations were apparent in their responses:

- *See if the phenomenon happens or make a phenomenon happen*: empirical investigation as an unproblematic process of finding out 'what actually happens', or of intervention in a phenomenon in order to observe the outcome.
- *Relate cause and effect*: empirical investigation which requires an intervention to seek a cause or predict an outcome (often associated with producing socially useful findings).
- *Evaluate a theory*: empirical investigation as the collection of evidence in order to check, test or develop a model or theory or to compare theories.

See if the phenomenon happens or make a phenomenon happen

The criterion used by students for the question being scientific in this case was whether or not there is any observational evidence for the phenomenon occurring or whether such evidence can be found.

In some cases, the students argued that it was possible to test whether the particular phenomenon happens using direct observation as evidence. It was common, for example, for young people to think that questions such as 'How was the Earth made?', 'Is the Earth's atmosphere heating up?' and 'Which is the best diet to keep babies healthy?', could be answered in an unproblematic way through direct observation. A 9-year-old agreed that the question 'Is the Earth's atmosphere heating up?' was a scientific question. When asked, 'What made you decide that one was a scientific question?', the response was, 'Because sometimes they send people outside the Earth to see'. Similarly, for the question 'What diet is best to keep babies healthy?', a 9-year-old commented: 'They would see what food and that would keep it healthy and that and grow up to be a strong baby.'

In both cases, answers to the questions are seen as emerging in an obvious way from simple observations. In some cases, a simple intervention was involved: 'You could try it and see what happens'. Again, the criterion being used is observational evidence for an event occurring.

Relating cause and effect

This characterization of a scientific question is one which portrays science as seeking causes of events or predicting outcomes. Very often this is associated with an instrumental view of science, a view which portrays science as providing socially useful knowledge. This was particularly apparent in the questions 'How was the Earth made?', 'Is the Earth's atmosphere heating up?' and 'Which is the best diet to keep babies healthy?'. For example:

I What is it about that one that made you decide it was a scientific question?
S You've got to decide what's causing it. If it is heating up, then you've got to try and stop it by using different things like no CFCs . . .

('Is the Earth's atmosphere heating up?'; age 16)

I Why is that a scientific question?
S 'Cause there might be some form of chemical or vitamin that they don't know anything about that could improve babies' health that won't lead to diseases or anything like that.

('Which is the best diet to keep babies healthy?'; age 16)

In these examples, it is assumed that knowledge about causes is required in order to intervene in specific ways in the behaviour of phenomena or systems.

Evaluate a theory

This characterization involved reference to the testing of a theory. This was not a common type of response and, in the few cases where it occurred, the reference to the testing of a theory tended to be implicit rather than explicit. For example, in response to the question about babies' diet:

S We weren't absolutely sure about that, because it's like, it still comes under scientific questions as to which diet it is, because people have had to experiment in the past to try and see what different nutrients and stuff they need, to find out which diet is actually best. That's how we got baby food.

('Which is the best diet to keep babies healthy?'; age 16)

This student did not characterize the investigation in terms of simple empirical comparisons. Instead, she implied that an underlying theory about nutrition was required to address the question.

A more explicit reference to theory testing was made in response to the question 'How was the Earth made?':

S1 Yeah, well there's loads of theories to that. I mean, so-called the 'big bang' and it could have just been one planet exploding, right... Nobody actually knows how the Earth was made... I mean, they all say that some big meteor hit the Earth and spun it round the wrong way...

S2 Yeah. They're still looking for evidence in everything. You know, like digging up things. Fossils and everything.

('How was the Earth made?'; age 16)

This form of reasoning is characterized by a clear distinction being made between the description of the evidence on the one hand and the explanation or theory on the other. In a very few cases, evidence was seen to be used to evaluate competing theories.

Other responses

In addition to responses which reflected these representations of empirical investigation, some students, especially the younger ones, simply answered the question rather than judging it to be scientific or not. So, in response to the specific question 'Is it wrong to keep dolphins in captivity?', some students responded 'Yes, it is wrong to keep dolphins in captivity because it is cruel'. In the case of the older students, some simply assumed that it was obvious that the question was scientific without giving a justification for it.

I How was the Earth made? Why are they interested in that?

S They want to find out how it was made and what it's made out of.

('How was the Earth made?'; age 16)

This occurred even when the student's attention was refocused on the judgement for why they considered it to be a scientific question.

Age-related trends in representations of empirical testing

Overall, the students mentioned empirical testability less than other criteria for judging whether or not a question is scientific. The proportion of students' responses which referred to empirical testing as a criterion (shown

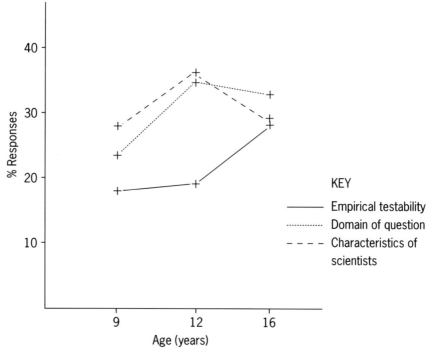

Figure 6.1 Proportion of responses using specified criterion for judging a question as scientific.

in Fig. 6.1) varied from 18 per cent at age 9 to 28 per cent at age 16. There was a statistically significant difference with age in the proportion of responses mentioning empirical testability as a feature of scientific questions ($p < 0.001$, χ^2). (The statistical test χ^2 was used throughout this study. Notes and an example are given in Appendix 1.)

The younger students were not particularly aware of the distinction between questions which were empirically testable and those which, for various reasons (involving for example, ethical judgements), were not. The older students were more conscious of whether or not a question could be operationalized for empirical investigation:

    I Okay. What made you feel like you didn't want to put it with
      scientific questions then?
    S Not really summat they can research. The ethics of it.
              ('Is it wrong to keep dolphins in captivity?'; age 16)

In addition to the older students mentioning empirical testability as a criterion for judging a question to be scientific more frequently than the younger students, the portrayal of what is involved in empirical testing also showed an age-related trend. Fig. 6.2 shows the trends with age in the

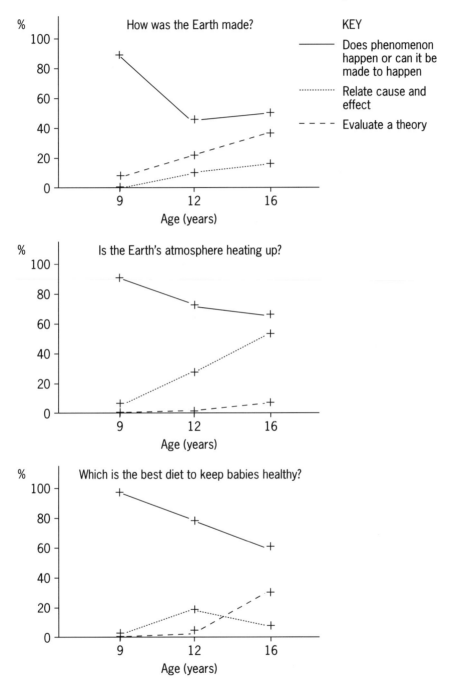

Figure 6.2 Proportion of responses using different representations of empirical testing.

types of empirical testing mentioned for three of the questions: 'How was the Earth made?', 'Is the Earth's atmosphere heating up? and 'Which is the best diet to keep babies healthy?'.

We are cautious about portraying the types of empirical testing which students refer to as a strict hierarchy, as different approaches to empirical testing may be appropriate in particular contexts. For this reason, we did not combine the results for the types of empirical testing across the questions.

As the graphs in Fig. 6.2 show, for each question there was a trend with age away from the view that scientific questions can be answered simply by looking, and towards the view that scientific questions address underlying mechanisms or theories. These trends are typical of those observed for the other questions. Nine-year-olds typically referred to scientific questions as being ones which involved an unproblematic process of finding out whether something really does happen, or can be made to happen. The older students, when they referred to empirical testing as a criterion for judging whether or not a question is scientific or not, tended more often to reflect a view of empirical testing as a search for relationships or mechanisms; for example, in order to stop global warming, it is necessary to know the cause of global warming as well as whether it is happening. In a small number of cases, the older students referred explicitly to an empirical process of data collection in order to evaluate a theory (such as a particular theory about how the Earth was made).

Overall, therefore, empirical testability was seen as a criterion for judging whether or not a question is scientific by an increasing proportion of students with age. There was also an age-related trend in the way that empirical testability was portrayed, with more of the younger students holding the view that scientific questions can be answered by direct observation and older students beginning to recognize scientific questions as addressing theories for explaining events.

The domain of the question

The domain of the question – both the type of subject matter involved and the perceived social importance of the question – was often referred to by young people in characterizing questions as being scientific or not.

The perceived subject matter of scientific questions

As we might expect, in many cases the students' ideas about what are scientific and unscientific subjects appeared to be grounded in their experience of school science, or popular representations of science in the media. The questions most commonly cited as relating to science were 'How was the Earth made?', 'Is the Earth's atmosphere heating up?', 'Which diet is best to keep babies healthy?', 'What kinds of bacteria are in the water supply?' and 'Can any metal be made into a magnet?'. By contrast, questions about TV programmes, ghosts and washing powder were often viewed as non-scientific. In the following response, we see a student judging a question to be scientific because the subject matter involves the human body:

I Do you think it would be interesting to the scientists?
S Well yes, because [it's] sort of studying science and bodies.
('Which is the best diet to keep babies healthy?'; age 16)

In the following example, the students appear to make their judgement on their perception of school subjects:

S1 Well washing powder . . . isn't that maths, isn't it?
S2 We do questions like that in maths.
('Is it cheaper to buy a large or a small packet of washing powder?'; age 16)

In most cases, the students judged whether or not the domain of the question was scientific by matching it with certain prototypical cases as in the example above involving mathematics. In a very small number of cases, we caught glimpses of students struggling towards expressing a view of scientific phenomena as being those which had an underlying replicability to them. This was not seen to be the case for social phenomena, where different people may hold different views, for example:

I Which is the best programme on TV?
S Oh that's a matter of opinion and it's . . . erm sort of it'd have to be carried out by market research. Erm it's not really scientific at all.
('Which is the best programme on TV?'; age 16)

Distinctions appeared to be drawn between ethical questions, social phenomena and the more regular and replicable phenomena that are thought to be scientific. It is interesting to note here that, although they are acquired for the most part in a tacit way, students' views on the kinds of domains that scientific questions address appear to be in broad agreement with those held by most people, both scientists and other adults.

The perceived social importance of scientific questions

Questions perceived as being of broad social relevance were often suggested to be scientific questions *for this reason*. The questions most commonly referred to in this way were 'Is the Earth's atmosphere heating up?', 'Which is the best diet to keep babies healthy?' and 'What kind of bacteria are in the water supply?'. In response to the question 'Which is the best diet to keep babies healthy?', a 9-year-old responded that a scientist would be interested in the question, 'So they [babies] don't get diarrhoea all the time . . . so they don't get poorly'. Similarly, scientists were seen to be interested in the question 'How was the Earth made?' because 'we need to stop pollution destroying it'.

There is a close similarity between these responses and those in the earlier section which refer to making a phenomenon happen. Responses were put in this category if the emphasis in the judgement was on social significance rather than on empirical testability. Although the social significance of a question was regularly cited as a reason for the question being a scientific question, the students did not classify questions with no perceived social relevance as non-scientific.

Age-related trends

The domain of the question was referred to as a basis for judging whether or not a question was scientific in about a quarter of the responses at age 9, increasing to over one-third at ages 12 and 16 (see Fig. 6.1). The difference in the proportion of responses referring to the domain of the question between ages 9 and 12 was statistically significant ($p < 0.003$, χ^2).

There were no clear age-related trends in the ways in which the domains of the questions were portrayed. However, responses which appeared to differentiate between social, economic and natural phenomena, or to exclude ethical questions, were noted only at age 16 among a small number of students.

The characteristics of scientific work

Many students drew upon images of scientists as individuals, and the particular institutional settings in which scientists work, in characterizing the sorts of questions that would be addressed by science. A spectrum of characterizations of scientists and the institutional settings in which they work was noted. These ranged from a stereotypical 'cartoon image' of the mad professor to a view of scientists as professionals with a variety of aims, working in a range of institutions (including hospitals and industrial laboratories).

Several examples of stereotyped views of scientists were apparent in the students' justifications of the types of questions that would be investigated in science:

S1 Scientific people won't bother with babies' food and things like that.
S2 'Cause they're . . .
S1 'Cause erm they're too busy working they won't bother with food and stuff.

> ('Which is the best diet to keep babies healthy?'; age 9)

I Okay. You didn't think that scientists would try and answer that question either. Why?
S Because if they've got wives their wives will be doing it.

> ('Is it cheaper to buy a large or a small packet of washing powder?'; age 9)

I   Okay. So why do you think scientists wouldn't be interested in it?
S   Because they don't watch telly much and there would just be some boring programmes and things like that, and they wouldn't really be interested in programmes and TV.

('Which is the best programme on TV?'; age 9)

In such cases where students did not differentiate between the personal and professional interests of scientists, questions relating to matters perceived as 'worldly' or 'feminine', such as TV programmes, washing powder or babies, were not viewed as scientific questions. This sort of characterization of scientists was used by a number of 9-year-olds, but was rarely noted at ages 12 and 16.

In the two older age groups, the students placed more emphasis upon the professional rather than personal interests of scientists. This is illustrated in the examples given in the previous section about the domains of scientific questions. Scientists were seen as interested in addressing socially important questions rather than personal and idiosyncratic ones. In some cases, the students' responses reflected fairly narrow definitions of the professional groups who are seen to be engaged in scientific work:

I   You weren't sure about that one either.
S   No they'd leave it up to the dietitians and that don't they at hospitals.

('Which is the best diet to keep babies healthy?'; age 16)

In a small number of cases, the responses of 16-year-olds hinted at a more sophisticated and differentiated portrayal of scientific work, with scientists being seen as working collaboratively and in different kinds of institutional settings.

The perceived characteristics of scientific work were used as a criterion for classifying a question as being a scientific question or not in about one-third of the responses at all ages. There was no trend with age in the proportion of students using this as a criterion. As we have already mentioned, however, the characteristics of scientists and scientific work which were portrayed did change with age, with the stereotypical image of the scientist being largely restricted to the 9-year-old age group.

Summary: young people's characterizations of the purposes of science

In this chapter, we have considered an aspect of how young people characterize scientific activity and distinguish it from other activities. We did this by asking students to consider a range of questions and to judge those they considered to be scientific or not scientific, giving their reasons. The responses given by the young people reflected three features of their portrayal of science:

- whether or not a question could be investigated empirically;
- whether the domain of the question related to a subject area which was

seen as prototypically a science domain, involving physical or biological phenomena;
- whether the activity was in keeping with the perceived personal and institutional characteristics of scientific work.

All three features were represented in students' responses at all three ages with the older students using more criteria in making a judgement. The proportion of students who used the criterion of whether or not a question could be investigated empirically increased from 17 per cent at age 9 to nearly 30 per cent at age 16. There was also a significant change between the ages of 9 and 12 years in the proportion of students referring to the domain of the question as a criterion. The other feature was mentioned by about one-third of the students at all ages. There were also age-related trends in the type of responses which characterized the students' portrayals within each of the three features.

Empirical testing	The younger students tended to characterize empirical testing as a simple process of observation from which outcomes would be obvious. The older students seemed to be more aware that empirical testing may involve finding out about mechanisms or testing theories.
Domain of enquiry	There were few age-related trends in this feature. Students of all ages tended to view scientific domains as including physical and biological phenomena and excluding social phenomena. The younger students tended to draw on school science experiences to make their judgements, whereas the older students drew on a wider range of experiences. They were also beginning to be aware of some issues (e.g. ethical ones) not being amenable to scientific enquiry.
Characteristics of scientific work	Many younger students referred to a stereotyped image of scientists and made no distinction between their personal and professional concerns. At ages 12 and 16, most young people viewed scientists as addressing important problems of social relevance. A small number of 16-year-olds indicated that scientific work is collaborative and can take place in a range of settings (hospitals, industrial laboratories, fieldwork).

As a final comment, it is important to indicate that although there were trends in the results from the cohorts across the age groups, at the individual level there was little evidence of students at any age being able to articulate a general characterization of what constitutes a scientific question, or of using particular representations of science in consistent ways across the range of questions.

7 | Students' views of the nature and status of scientific knowledge

Introduction

This chapter presents findings on the second of the key features addressed by the research study, namely, students' views on the *nature and status of scientific knowledge*. The study focused on three strands of this epistemological dimension in students' representations of science: what young people see as characterizing scientific enquiry, their views on the nature and status of scientific theories and the relationship between theories and evidence.

In presenting an account of these three strands of students' epistemological reasoning, this chapter draws on evidence from students' responses to four probes: **Experiment, Theory Stories, Warrants for Belief** and **Theory and Evidence.**

Students' views on what constitutes scientific forms of enquiry

In Chapter 3, we argued for a broad interpretation of scientific enquiry as involving the collection and use of data or evidence. There are situations when such data are used in providing the accounts of phenomena in the natural world which require explanation; in other situations, data are used to test proposed theories or explanations. Experimentation, as a planned intervention in a phenomenon, is thus a particular form of scientific enquiry. However, since the term 'experiment' is so widely used in school science, often with a meaning that encompasses any practical activity, we thought that it would be informative to find out what

Table 7.1 Statements presented in the **Experiment** probe.

Name	Statement on card	Comment
'Cake'	This person is making a cake, by following a recipe. They will measure out all the ingredients, mix them together, and bake the cake.	Practical activity, outcome known; little suggestion of science in context
'Crystal'	This person is following some instructions given on a worksheet by the teacher, to make some large crystals of salt.	Practical activity, outcome known; stronger suggestion of science in context
'Radio'	This person has just switched the radio on, but it did not work. They are now finding out why the radio won't work.	Practical activity, outcome unknown; little suggestion of science in context
'Towel'	This person is finding out which one of the three paper towels is best at mopping up water.	Practical activity, outcome unknown; stronger suggestion of science in context
'Post'	This person works at the post office. He is weighing parcels to decide which stamps the customer needs to buy.	Measurement, no suggestion of underpinning theory
'Rain'	This person has a hunch that there is usually more rain in April than in September. They are keeping a diary of the weather each day to see if their hunch is right.	Empirical evaluation of formally stated hypothesis
'Dissolve'	This person has an idea that the smaller the grains in sugar, the quicker it will dissolve in water, and is testing the idea.	Empirical evaluation of formally stated hypothesis
'Conduct'	This person has an idea that electricity will go through *all* metals, but it only goes through a few things that are not metals. She is testing this idea.	Empirical evaluation of formally stated hypothesis
'Balloons'	When the bottle is heated, the balloon fills with air. This could be because the air *expands* when heated, or because hot air rises. This person is heating the bottle upside down to find out which idea is best.	Empirical evaluation of explanatory theory

representations students of different ages have of the activity described by the term 'experiment'.

The **Experiment** probe was designed to require students to elaborate on what they considered to be involved in an experiment. Pairs of students were presented with nine cards, each of which carried a description of a particular practical activity. The students were asked to examine and discuss the statements on the cards and to classify each activity as 'an experiment', 'not an experiment' or 'not sure', giving their reasons. The statements on the nine cards are given in Table 7.1.

The activities presented on the cards were selected to include situations with no apparent theoretical or investigational component (for example, following a recipe to make a cake), as well as situations in which data of some kind are collected in order to evaluate a stated hypothesis (for example, finding the time it takes crystals of different sizes to dissolve in order to check an idea). Furthermore, some contexts were chosen as representing everyday-type activities (for example, 'Radio'), whereas other activities were chosen because of their likely associations with school science (for example, 'Conduct'). The students' responses were analysed with a view to answering the following questions:

- What do students see as being the purpose of experimentation?

- What do they see as characterizing the process of experimentation?

Representations of forms of enquiry involved in experimentation

One of the main reasons which students gave to justify their classification was whether or not the activity was considered to be investigative in some way; that is, whether or not it required some kind of 'finding out'. A number of distinct representations for what is involved in 'finding out' were apparent in students' discussions and these reflected features similar to those found for the empirical investigation strand of the **Scientific Questions** probe (see chapter 6). Four types of representation were identified: (1) any practical activity; (2) making a phenomenon happen or finding something new; (3) relating cause and effect; and (4) evaluating a theory. These are discussed in turn.

Activity

The simplest representation of an experiment was anything that involved some sort of physical action or practical activity, including activities such as measuring, mixing and even including cases such as baking a cake.

Making a phenomenon happen or finding something new

From this point of view, an experiment involves an intervention of some sort in which something new is made to happen, or which produces new information about the behaviour of the phenomenon. Some students argued that baking a cake or making a crystal of salt could be an experiment if the person was doing it for the first time, or in a new way, and did not know how it would turn out. For example, in the 'Rain' activity, two 16-year-old students argued:

S1 Yeah, 'cause you've got to experiment and see how much rainfall there is, because that's how the weather reporters know it.
S2 They do it for the weather reports
I OK, when you say you have to experiment to figure out, what do you mean by experiment?
S1 Graphs.
I OK.
S2 To see how much it rained.

('Rain'; age 16)

In this case, it appeared to be the unknown outcome, in terms of finding out the specific rainfall figures, which characterized the activity as an experiment.

Relating cause and effect

This characterization of an experiment involves a clear investigative component, usually a comparison of conditions as they affect an outcome. For example, in the case of the 'Dissolve' activity:

I What makes that one an experiment?
S 'Cause they are seeing if smaller grains will dissolve quickly, than bigger grains of sugar ... They would get lumps of sugar and really, really ground-up sugar and then put them in water or tea, or something, but you have got to be able to see through it, and see which one dissolves the quickest.

('Dissolve'; age 12)

In this case, the experiment is being characterized in terms of a comparison of outcomes (the time taken for sugar to dissolve) for different initial conditions (different sizes of grains of sugar). As we will show later, this portrayal of an experiment as a comparison of conditions as they affect an outcome was a dominant view across different contexts at all three ages. We suspect that this may be, in part at least, a consequence of 'fair tests' being emphasized in school science investigations in the UK as a result of the introduction of the National Curriculum.

Evaluating a theory

This characterization goes beyond relating conditions to outcomes and involves the empirical evaluation of theories, hypotheses or generalizations. In response to the activity 'Conduct', a 16-year-old stated: 'Well she's thought of an idea and then she's decided to test it and see whether it's right.' About the 'Balloon' activity, a 16-year-old said: 'Well they're trying different ways to find out which statement's true – whether air expands ... well ... why the balloon blows up 'cause of whether air expands or whether hot air rises.' This representation of an experiment requires the student to recognize the existence of an idea or theory which is to be evaluated. It was interesting to note that a small number of students even rejected some of the activities which involved fair testing as being experiments because there was no theory to be tested. One 16-year-old commented about 'Towel':

S It could be an experiment but then it couldn't be as well.
I OK. In what way is it like an experiment to you?
S They are trying to find out which one's the best . . . which one dissolves the water the quickest.
I OK. And why is it not like an experiment?
S It's not like any of these, where they are testing out an idea.

('Towel', aged 16)

Age-related trends

The prevalence of the different representations showed a clear trend with age, with a decrease in the proportion of students portraying an experiment as making a phenomenon happen and an increase in the proportion who referred to experiments as evaluating a theory. This is illustrated for three of the activities: 'Balloon', 'Dissolve' and 'Conduct' (see Fig. 7.1). These were chosen because, unlike other activities in the set, they had the potential to be seen as involving the evaluation of a theory or generalization. It is therefore of particular interest to note the proportion of responses at each of the three ages which did not refer directly or indirectly to theory evaluation for these three activities, but instead portrayed the activity as relating cause and effect, as the following excerpt relating to the balloon activity illustrates:

I And the balloons and air one. What was it about that, that made you decide it was an experiment?
S Well, 'cause you've got two different ways, and they're just testing to see which one it is.
I Right so it's er, it's different ways of getting the balloon to rise.
S Experimenting.

('Balloons'; age 16)

In this case, experimentation is being seen as determining which initial condition (orientation of the bottle) results in the balloon becoming inflated. In the following example, by contrast, the purpose of the activity is seen as testing alternative hypotheses.

I Can you describe what that would tell them about what happens when the one upside down . . .
S Blows up the balloon.
I What's he trying to find out?
S If it blows up the balloon then air expands when it's hot, not rises.

('Balloons'; age 16)

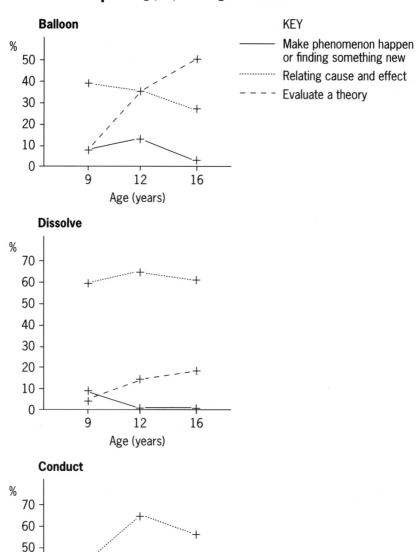

Figure 7.1 Prevalence of different representations of experimentation.

The number of responses at ages 9, 12 and 16 referring to evaluation of the two theories in the activity 'Balloon' increased with age. The description of this activity given on the card *explicitly* referred to 'finding out which idea is the best' and yet many students (especially the younger ones) frequently did *not* refer to this in justifying their responses. We are not suggesting that younger children *cannot* respond in terms of evaluating ideas, but simply that very often they do not do so.

The percentage of responses which categorized 'Dissolve' and 'Conduct' as experiments because they involved the evaluation of a theory was lower at each age than for 'Balloons', but once again there was an increased use of this representation in the oldest age group.

Representations of forms of enquiry: a review

The types of representations found in students' responses to the **Experiment** probe were strikingly similar to those found in the empirical processes strand of students' responses to the **Scientific Questions** probe (see chapter 6).

Some student reasoning about these two tasks contained no element of enquiry at all. This was the case for the responses to **Scientific Questions** where students, despite probing, simply answered the question, rather than judging whether or not it was a scientific question. There appeared to be no sense in which the question, as given, was seen as an object which could be extracted for consideration and evaluation from the flow of discourse. Similarly, some student responses to the **Experiment** probe included no mention of an element of enquiry but characterized an experiment as any physical activity.

In the majority of cases, however, students' responses to **Scientific Questions** and **Experiment** incorporated an element of enquiry. Three main representations of forms of enquiry were apparent in the students' responses: (1) making a phenomenon happen or finding something new; (2) relating cause and effect; and (3) evaluating a theory.

Not only were the types of responses similar but, as a comparison of Figs 6.2 and 7.1 shows, in both cases we see similar trends with age, with an increase in the prevalence of responses which portray scientific enquiry as involving the evaluation of a theory. In both cases, however, this form of response was still in the minority even among 16-year-old students, with one of the other representations predominating at all ages.

Students' views of the nature of explanation in science

A central aim of science is to provide explanations for natural phenomena. In some cases, explanations take the form of generalizations or laws. Events are 'explained' if they can be deduced logically from the generalization or law. The development of theories or theoretical models provides what may be considered a more fundamental approach to explaining phenomena in the world. Events in the real world are seen as the consequence of the properties and behaviour of entities in the theoretical model – they are 'explained' by them. The nature and status of theoretical models, and the ways they are seen to relate to, and be constrained by, phenomena in the real world, has been and continues to be the subject of discussion and dispute among philosophers and sociologists of science. A review of some of the different positions on this matter was presented in Chapter 3.

Here, our focus is on students' views of the nature of explanation in science, specifically their representations of what constitutes a scientific theory and their grounds for accepting a scientific claim to be true. These issues were explored using two probes: **Theory Stories** and **Warrants for Belief.**

Although we find it useful to distinguish between explanations which are generalizations and those which are theories, this does not mean that students make this distinction. The term 'theory' is the one that is commonly used in science lessons and therefore we thought it appropriate to use this term in probing students' representations of explanation in science.

Theory Stories

This probe was designed to find out what meanings students attribute to the word 'theory', and to explore how students characterize scientific theories and their relation to evidence. To provide a context for students to talk about theories, a number of short stories were written, involving young people talking about a 'theory' and the evidence that might support it. A number of stories were drafted and trialled. Three stories were finally selected, relating to the rusting of iron, the behaviour of air on heating and the germ theory of decay. These incorporated 'theories' which the youngest students could understand and contexts which were familiar to students at all three ages. (The text of the stories and the interview protocol are given in Appendix 2.)

The 'Rusting' and 'Germs' stories were structured so that a phenomenon was observed by a pair of characters; then one character gave a possible explanation for the phenomenon, using the words 'I have a theory about that . . .'. After reading this part of the story, the interviewer then asked the students what they thought the character meant by 'a theory' and probed whether the students had any idea what the theory might be. The story continued with the character's theory, and at the end of the story the interviewer asked the students the questions: 'Can the characters can be sure that the theory is correct?' and 'What could be done to prove that the theory is correct?'

The story about the behaviour of air on heating ('Balloons') was slightly different in structure. The characters in the story outline two different theories to explain why a balloon, when fixed over the end of a glass bottle, inflates when the bottle is heated. As well as asking the students about the meaning of the word 'theory' and whether the characters can be sure that the theory is correct, the interviewer also asked 'which theory is best to explain the evidence available in the story?'

The probe was administered to pairs of students, each pair being asked about all three stories. The interviewer first explained that they were going to look at some short stories, all about theories. The interviews began with the 'Rusting' story, then the 'Balloons' story and, finally, the 'Germs' story. The stories were printed and read aloud, the printed copy being on the table for the students to follow. The printed text was organized with the interviewer's questions at the end of a page, so that the students answered questions without seeing what came next in the story.

The analysis of students' responses focused on the following questions:

- What do students consider the status of scientific theories to be?
- How do they consider theories relate to phenomena?
- To what extent do they see theories and laws as conjectural?

Meaning of the word 'theory'

Those students who said they knew what the word 'theory' meant ascribed one of the following four meanings to the word:

Vague idea; knowing something
In some cases, the students simply stated that a theory involves knowing something about the situation but offered no more elaboration. As one 9-year-old said, 'A theory is . . . an idea'.

Prediction
A theory was described as meaning an idea as to what might happen in a situation: 'Like what she thinks'll happen when she does it' (12-year-old referring to the 'Balloon's story).

Contextual explanation
In some cases, the students responded by stating a possible explanation in the presented context, rather than explaining what a theory is in general terms. For example, in response to the 'Rusting' story, one 9-year-old said: 'Does it mean . . . it's because the water is making it rusty when it splashes up the wall?' Such responses do indicate some awareness that theories are meant to explain phenomena even though this is not stated explicitly.

General explanation
A small number of 9-year-olds and a majority of the 16-year-olds stated that theories are explanations of what is happening. Their responses indicated

a general view of the word 'theory' rather than a meaning bound to one of the stories. For example, one 16-year-old in response to the 'Rusting' story said: 'He thinks he knows why . . . why it's happened . . . why the railings at the seaside are a lot rustier than the ones at school . . . make a conclusion'.

Overall, a minority of the 9-year-olds, about two-thirds of the 12-year-olds and nearly all of the 16-year-olds said they knew what the word 'theory' meant. Theory was described as a vague idea about something by about a third of the 9- and 12-year-olds but few of the 16-year-olds. The word 'theory' as a prediction or contextualized explanation was used by a minority of students at all ages. The main trend was the growth in the use of the word to mean a generalized explanation (i.e. one which could be stated independently of the specific context) from less than a quarter of the 9-year-olds to over three-quarters of the 16-year-olds.

Representations of scientific theories

Three main representations of the nature of theories were identified in the students' responses.

Description of phenomenon

This form of representation of the nature of theories involves no element of empirical evaluation. A theory is portrayed as an unproblematic feature of common knowledge: it is a taken-for-granted 'fact' about how things are. In discussing the 'Germs' story, for example, a 16-year-old commented that you could be sure that milk goes off because microbes grow better when it's warm, because 'When you put them in the fridge it doesn't get rid of them. It just . . . they don't grow as quickly'. Since this representation of theory is a taken-for-granted statement of how the world is (in this case, the microbes in milk make it go sour), the theory is not problematized and no distinction is thus made between theory and evidence.

Explanation as correlating variables

In this form of reasoning, scientific theories involve relating variables. This representation recognizes the distinction between theory and evidence. The theory, however, is portrayed as a correlation between stated variables, and the aim of the empirical evaluation is to 'prove' or demonstrate that the stated variables do in fact influence the phenomenon in question (for example, that salt speeds up the rusting process), without any reference to underlying mechanisms. In response to the 'Germs' story, a pair of 16-year-old students stated that they were sure that the theory that germs grow better in the warm than the cold was correct:

> S1 We've already done experiments . . . we had some milk left out and some milk put in the fridge and dipped our fingers in them and took down the results and that's what we ended up with. It went off quicker in the heat.

I I see.
S2 We put it in the freezer, right, and they don't do anything 'cos it's
too cold for them.

('Germs'; age 16)

As this example illustrates, this portrayal of theory is one of establishing
relations between features of phenomena (in this case, the temperature
of the milk and whether it goes sour) which are observable or taken as
existing. It is also striking that the entities proposed by the scientific theory
– in this case the germs – are taken for granted. This representation of
theory allows for different variables to be considered as possibly influential. However, the underlying position is that only one relationship is true
and that the choice of variables to consider, and to exclude as irrelevant,
is obvious and embodies no prior conceptual commitment. In some cases,
this portrayal includes establishing a linear causal sequence between a
variable which initiates a change in a system and which, through a chain
of intermediate variables, links to an outcome. For example, in the case of
the 'Balloons' story, it was common for students to argue using the causal
sequence: heat makes the air in the vessel rise and hence the balloon blows
up.

Modelling
In this form of reasoning, theory is seen as involving a modelling process.
The portrayal of theory and its relation to evidence involves positing a theoretical system or model and then relating the properties of this model to
observed changes in the system to be explained. Theories are thus clearly
differentiated from evidence: they involve entities of a different type from
those observed directly. These formal or theoretical entities are understood within the context of a theory, and it is their position and function
within the theory that gives them meaning. Furthermore, because theories
are underdetermined by observational data, alternative possible models
or theories can, in principle at least, be entertained.

This more sophisticated portrayal of scientific theory was less apparent
in the students' responses, and the notion that theories are conjectures
with a provisional status was hinted at in the responses of very few students indeed, even at age 16.

In the following example, 16-year-old students are discussing the 'Balloons' story, and in doing so introduce the notion of air molecules whose
behaviour they use to model, and hence explain, the behaviour of air on
heating. Their discussion, although it incorporates what would be considered to be scientifically incorrect statements, does portray the modelling
of the phenomenon in terms of theoretical entities. In the discussion, the
students also make predictions based on the behaviour of these entities and
check them against observations. (In the following section of the discussion, the students go on to consider theories which explain why the balloon
expands when the vessel is inverted.)

S1 The air molecules are still being heated and have got all the energy and are moving about just as much as they were before when it was the right way up.

S2 She's right (referring to the girl in the story) that hot air does rise . . . it's just that other things happen as well so . . . The hot air would still be going to the top of the tin and then cooling and pouring down, back down, again because of the. . . .

S1 Yeah. But it also happens that the particles jiggle around and expand. So (it still fills).

S2 Yeah.

('Balloons'; age 16)

Age-related trends in views of the nature of theory

The word 'theory' was understood by an increasing proportion of students to mean a generalized explanation, with a majority holding this view by age 16. The most common portrayal was in terms of correlating specific variables. There was a small, but not statistically significant, increase with age in the proportion of students who portrayed a theory as a model, with about 20 per cent of 16-year-old students reasoning in this way. There was very little evidence indeed that students appreciated the conjectural nature of theories (although this may have been a consequence of the examples we chose for discussion). For the majority of students, theories appear to be composed of entities (and variables) which map on to events in the world in an unproblematic way. Trends in the characterization of the nature of theory are shown in Fig. 7.2 for two contexts.

Warrants for Belief

A central claim of science is that it produces reliable knowledge about the natural world. Indeed, from a commonsense point of view, 'scientific knowledge is proven knowledge' (Chalmers 1982:3). To assert, or agree to, a statement about the natural world is to declare a belief. But, as we have argued in Chapter 2, belief is not the same as knowledge. From a philosophical point of view, if someone asserts something, then that is their belief. Only if they can provide reasons for their belief can it be regarded as knowledge. This distinction is an important one in education where rote learning, the mere acquisition of beliefs, is disparaged; instead, the aim is acquisition of knowledge, which includes grounds for beliefs.

The extent to which students in this study could articulate the evidence on which they accepted certain scientific claims was explored in the **Warrants for Belief** probe. The probe explored the reasons that students gave for accepting two specific scientific statements as true. These statements were:

- The Earth is round like a very large ball.
- A bulb in a circuit lights because electricity goes from the battery, through the wires, and to the bulb.

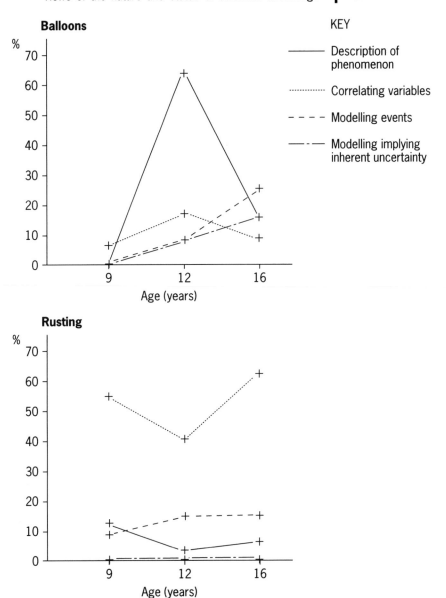

Figure 7.2 Prevalence of different representations of the nature of theory for the 'Balloons' and 'Rusting' cases.

Almost all students at ages 9, 12 and 16 said that they had heard of both these ideas and regarded them as true. The interview then centred on their reasons for accepting the ideas as true, or correct. The analysis of responses focused on the following question:

> What types of warrants (if any) are drawn upon by students to justify their acceptance or rejection of theories?

Some students seemed unable to consider the possibility of the Earth being other than spherical, or to separate the phenomenon of a bulb lighting from an explanation of it. For these students, the issue of warrants for belief did not arise. Responses of this sort were coded as 'observation and explanation not distinguished'. Other responses fell into two main categories: *warrants involving evidence* and *warrants based on acceptance of authority*.

Warrants involving evidence

Direct perceptual evidence
A common response at all ages was that reliable knowledge is necessarily based on direct perceptual evidence. Photographs from space were mentioned by many students. A considerable number, including some 16-year-olds, appeared to think that the Earth has been known to be spherical only since the launch of the first satellites in the 1950s!

I So what makes you believe the Earth's round?
S Satellite pictures.
I Satellite pictures . . . Do you think that before then (taking the pictures) people thought the Earth was round?
S No. They probably just thought it was flat then . . . They used to think you'd fall off the edge of the Earth.

('Earth'; age 16)

In the electricity context, lightning was mentioned as an example of 'seeing' electricity moving:

I   Okay, you have never actually seen electricity, how come that you believe that it is moving in the wire?
S1 Well, we have seen electricity, when lightning strikes.
I   Lightning. Okay, and so you think there is like lightning in the wire?
S1 Yeah.
S2 Sort of, yeah, 'cause lightning is electricity.

('Electricity'; aged 9)

Inferences from evidence
Some students, however, appeared able to locate the given proposition within a wider framework of understanding of the phenomenon. For

example, if the Earth is a planet similar to other cosmic bodies, then it is likely to be the same shape:

I   Okay, so why do you believe the Earth's round?
S1 Well, when people go into space they look back at the world and it's round.
S2 You know like the Moon seems round as well.

('Earth'; age 16)

A small number of responses, mainly from older students, appealed to inferences from indirect evidence, such as objects disappearing over the horizon, and the apparent motion of Sun, Moon and stars.

Technological efficacy
A few students of all ages argued that the technological efficacy of the idea provided grounds for acceptance; the existence of televisions and other working electrical gadgets provided support for the electricity statement, and the success of rocketry and space exploration for the astronomical one.

S1 ... and the same fact that we've been taught and built all kinds of stuff like a torch and rockets from the same sort of idea.
S2 If it weren't there it wouldn't work.
S1 So if that idea weren't true, then those things wouldn't happen.
S2 But ... so it's got to be there really.

('Electricity' and 'Earth'; age 16)

Warrants based on acceptance of authority

Blind authority
Many students at all ages cited the views of an authority figure as a warrant for belief. In many cases, nothing was added to explain how the authority figure could come to have the knowledge in question:

S You don't know for yourself. You just have to take someone else's word for it.
I And how do they know?
S It all comes from the man who discovered electricity.
   (...)
I It doesn't bother you that you can't see it going through the wires?
S No. Not really. There are some things that you just have to accept.

('Electricity'; age 16)

Reasons for accepting the authority
Some responses included implicit or explicit reasons for placing trust in authority sources. These ranged from discussing how the idea in question was supported by evidence which the authority possessed, to providing an evaluation of the information or an evaluation of the authority source itself:

S1 It all makes sense.
S2 Yeah.
I 'Cause it makes sense.
S2 Yeah.
    (...)
I And you said you were introduced to these ideas in school in science lessons ...
S2 And it makes more sense than any of the others.

('Electricity'; age 16)

S You know when a teacher's explaining and they show you these experiments?
I Yes.
S .... the proper teachers, you know like they learn about it all the time?
I Yes.
S Just like people say that the world's going to end and that lot and sometimes you don't believe that.
I And what makes you not believe it?
S Because of the way they talk. They go on to a different subject all the time when someone, you know, answers them and that, and they don't know what it's about.

('Electricity'; aged 12)

General patterns in students' responses

In considering the overall picture of students' responses, it is useful to divide the warrants based on evidence into two categories: those using direct perceptual evidence only, and those citing more complex links between evidence and the given idea. Similarly, warrants based on authority fall into two groups: those based on blind acceptance of authority, and those which also provide some reasons for accepting the authority.

For the statement about the round Earth, considerably more students at all ages gave warrants based on evidence than on authority. Most of their responses, however, were based on unsophisticated forms of reasoning, appealing to direct evidence or blindly accepting authority. Only 10 per cent of 9-year-olds gave responses based on the more sophisticated forms of evidence or authority reasoning. By age 16, this had risen to 30 per cent. There was a statistically significant difference ($p < 0.005$, χ^2) between ages 9 and 12 in the proportion of warrants based on more sophisticated forms of reasoning about evidence.

For the electricity statement, about 50 per cent of 9- and 12-year-olds appeared not to be able to distinguish clearly between the phenomenon of a bulb lighting and its explanation in terms of a 'flow of electricity'. Of the students who did offer warrants for accepting the explanatory statement, more appealed to evidence than to authority at all ages. The number

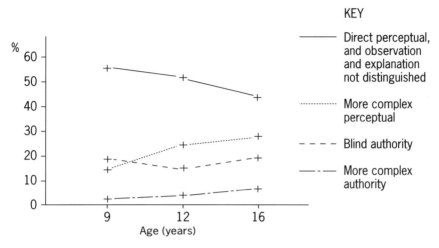

Figure 7.3   Prevalence of different types of **Warrants for Belief.**

of warrants using more sophisticated reasoning about evidence or authority increased significantly between ages 12 and 16. Even by age 16, however, only 40 per cent of warrants offered fell into this category.

The pattern of responses offered by children at the three ages is summarized in Fig. 7.3.

| Students' evaluation of theories

While there is fairly general agreement that science involves a complex interplay between evidence (from observation and experiment) and theory, there is, as Chapter 3 makes clear, considerable disagreement about the precise nature of the interrelationship. Few would now see theory as emerging solely from the collected data in a field of enquiry. An imaginative and creative step is involved in proposing a theory. The resulting theory is a conjecture, consistent with the available data, but going beyond it and not deducible from it. A central characteristic of science, in this view, is its particular approach to the checking and testing of proposed theories. Predictions from the theory are compared with empirical data. If there is agreement, then confidence in the theory is increased. If there is disagreement, then further work is needed. In this section of the chapter, we focus on how students evaluate theories using empirical evidence. We are interested in finding out the extent to which students can use evidence in logical and consistent ways to evaluate theories presented in science. The question of the extent to which students see this process as central to scientists' work in developing successful theories in science is also of interest, though a more difficult and subtle issue to investigate.

The ways in which students coordinate theory and evidence in the evaluation of theories has been the subject of a number of recent investigations.

An important study in this area by Kuhn *et al.* (1988) was reported in Chapter 4. In their study, students were presented with tasks concerning contrived situations in which several possible variables could affect an outcome. In one case, the task involved information on a number of dietary variables presented as binary choices – for example, fruit (apples or oranges), potato (baked or chips) – and their relation to whether or not groups of children did or did not catch a cold. A second context concerned properties of tennis balls and their relationship (if any) to the quality of serves. Kuhn and her colleagues were interested in the ways in which students reasoned about whether a variable does or does not make a difference to the outcome. From the results of their study (which are reported more fully in Chapter 4), Kuhn *et al.* drew strong conclusions about the development of what they term 'scientific thinking skills', which are seen as the skills of coordination of theory (their term; Kuhn *et al*, 1988: 219ff.), and evidence. They report their findings as showing that these skills develop with age and experience.

So the tasks used by Kuhn *et al.* were based on situations in which students had to link dichotomous variables to outcomes. There must be a question as to whether it is legitimate to call the logical reasoning skills involved in these tasks 'scientific thinking skills'. Explanations in science are not only based on associations between variables. This view of 'scientific thinking' captures, at best, only a portion of the reasoning involved in testing a theoretical model against experience.

Our **Theory and Evidence** probe bore some similarity in structure to the instrument used by Kuhn and her colleagues, but differed from it in two important respects:

- The contexts chosen related to scientific theories likely to be familiar to the students from school science, rather than artificially constructed ones.
- In one of the chosen contexts, the explanations considered took the form of a theoretical model; the students therefore had to make deductions from the model in order to arrive at specific predictions, which could then be compared with observation data. This involves all the steps involved in testing a scientific explanation against evidence, unlike explanations based on generalizations or causal models which involve only some of these steps.

Design and administration of the probe

After initial piloting in a range of contexts, the two areas chosen for the study were 'Electric circuits' and 'Floating and sinking'. The structure of the probe is outlined in Fig. 7.4.

There were a number of steps in the administration of this probe. In the case of the 'Electric circuits' context, the students were first reminded of some key observations which were both presented on a card and demonstrated to them (these are summarized in Fig. 7.5). In the case of the

Reminders about relevant phenomena

Remind students about the context and the class of phenomena involved.
For 'Electric circuits', specific observations were presented;
for 'Floating and sinking', verbal reminders were given.

Present alternative explanations

List of alternative explanations for the range of phenomena presented on a
card. The students were asked to select the explanation they thought best.

Presentation of evidence

Pieces of evidence for which the chosen explanation might be expected to
account, were presented in turn. The students were asked to consider each
piece of evidence in the light of their chosen explanation and to discuss
implications of consistency or inconsistency between evidence and explanation.

Figure 7.4 Outline structure of **Theory and Evidence** probe.

1 A single light bulb connected by two wires to
  a dry cell lights up.

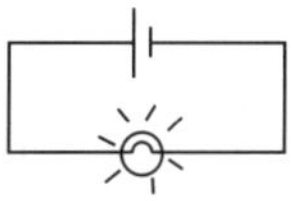

2 If the positive terminal of a dry cell is connected,
  by a single lead, to one terminal of a light bulb,
  the bulb does not light.

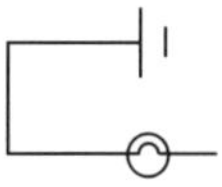

3 If the negative terminal of a dry cell is connected,
  by a single lead, to one terminal of a light bulb,
  the bulb does not light.

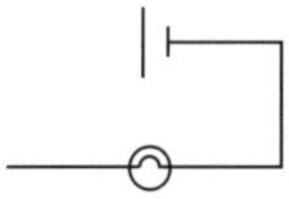

4 If the circuit for observation 1 above is kept connected for some time,
  the bulb will become dimmer and dimmer and will eventually go out. The
  dry cell is then 'flat' and cannot be used to light a bulb any longer.

Figure 7.5 Key observations presented to students before they chose the
'best explanation' for the behaviour of a simple electric circuit.

'Electric circuits'   'Floating and sinking'

Explanations of how a bulb lights in a simple circuit:

1 Electricity goes from one end of the battery along one wire to the bulb. It is used up in the bulb.
2 Electricity goes along both the wires *from* the battery *to* the bulb. This makes the bulb light.
3 Electricity goes along one wire from the battery to the bulb. Some of it is used up by the bulb. The leftover electricity goes back along the other wire to the battery.
4 Electricity goes along one wire from the battery to the bulb, through the bulb and back round to the battery.

Pieces of evidence

These were presented on cards, and also demonstrated using laboratory apparatus:

a We add a second bulb, identical to the first. Both bulbs light up, with the same brightness. But they are dimmer than the one bulb was when connected on its own. 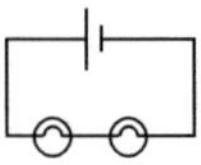
b We add a third bulb, identical to the first two. All three bulbs light up, with the same brightness. But they are dimmer than the two bulbs were, and much dimmer than the one bulb was. 
c We put two meters into the circuit to measure the electric current. The pointers on the two meters show exactly the same reading. The current is the same in both wires. 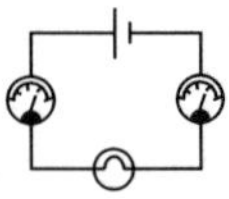
d We leave circuit c switched on for some time. The readings on the meters both get gradually smaller and eventually become zero. But they are always the same as each other.

Explanations of why some things float and others sink

1 Things which are light float. Things which are heavy sink.
2 Things float if they contain air. If they don't contain any air, they sink.
3 Some 'stuff' floats and anything made of it floats. Other 'stuff' sinks and anything made of it sinks. The 'stuff' it is made from is all that matters.

Pieces of evidence

These were presented in groups on cards, with illustrative diagrams:

a A toy boat floats
A toy car sinks
b A sheet of cooking foil sinks
A crumpled ball of cooking foil sinks
A boat made from cooking foil floats
c A glass bottle floats
A glass marble sinks
d A steel block sinks
A tiny pin (made of steel) sinks
A ship (made of steel) floats
A diving bell (made of steel) sinks
c A large ball of plasticene sinks
A small ball of plasticene sinks
A model boat made of plasticene floats
f A stone sinks
A candle floats
A potato sinks
A small piece of potato sinks

Figure 7.6 Explanations and evidence presented in the 'Electric circuits' and 'Floating and sinking' contexts.

'Floating and sinking' context, no initial observations were presented, as the students were clearly familiar with a wide range of instances from routine everyday experience. The remainder of the probe is summarized in Figure 7.6. The students were asked to select, from a list, their preferred explanation for the phenomenon in question. The explanations presented were drawn from what is known, from research, about children's ideas in these domains (for 'Electric circuits' see, for example, Shipstone 1985; for 'Floating and sinking' see Smith *et al.* 1984; Hewson 1986). In the case of the 'Electric circuits' context, the explanations were based on models of what might be going on in a circuit, whereas those for 'Floating and sinking' were based on generalizations from experience.

After the students had selected their preferred explanation, we asked them to predict what they thought would happen in each of a number of subsequent situations. The situations were then demonstrated to them and the students were asked to consider each piece of evidence in the light of their chosen explanation and to discuss the implications of consistency or inconsistency between evidence and explanation.

The students' responses to this probe were analysed at a number of levels. In this account, we first describe the types of responses given to the parts of the probe dealing with:

- the choice of explanation; and
- relating new evidence to a chosen explanation.

We then describe the general ways in which students appear to coordinate explanation and evidence and report trends with age in this feature of their reasoning.

In analysing the students' responses, we were interested in the following research questions:

> How do students think that theories are evaluated? Do they consider theories separately from the phenomena which they explain?
>
> Can students evaluate theories appropriately, using empirical evidence? Are they able to evaluate theories independently of their belief in the theory?

Choice of explanation

Consistent use of evidence and explanation

In the 'Electric circuits' context, some students at all ages used all the evidence presented appropriately and consistently in selecting an explanation. In the following example, 9-year-old students have chosen explanation 2, in which electricity goes along both wires from the battery to the bulb, and give an argued account of how it is in keeping with the key observations presented earlier:

I What was it about number two that you thought was best?
S1 Because if we had number four [continuous flow] electricity would go through this side, light the bulb for a few seconds and then go back and the bulb would go out.
I Go out again?
S1 Yes.
    (...)
I How about number three? The idea that electricity comes out. Some of it's used and then less goes back?
S1 Well, if you did that, when it ran out of electricity there wouldn't have been any more to use.
I Oh, you mean it had just run out of electricity?
S1 Yes.
S2 We think number two is the most powerful of them
    (...)
S1 It would last the shortest the batteries, but it would, the light would stop on more.
I The light would stay on more. I understand. How about number one? What didn't you like about that? The idea that electricity just goes out of one wire and then gets used up in the bulb.
S2 Because then you wouldn't need that wire.
I You wouldn't need the other wire. Okay.
S2 And it wouldn't work.

('Electric circuits'; age 9)

In this case, although the students seem to be using a model of a 'chunk' of electricity travelling round the circuit, they relate their knowledge of how the bulbs appear and the evidence presented in a way which is consistent with the theories.

In the 'Floating and sinking' context, where no specific pieces of evidence were presented before the students were asked to choose an explanation, it was interesting to note that many pairs drew on counter-examples from memory to reject some of the explanations presented. In such cases, the students often argued very systematically to a conclusion and, in so doing, showed an implicit understanding that one counter-example is enough to refute an explanation:

I OK. What do you think?
S1 Well we've thought of two things against one or two. [Referring to Explanations 1 and 2]
    (....)
I Okay. Tell me about one and two then. So what do you think against number one?

S2 Things which float are light. That's everything that sinks are heavy.
   Things that float aren't always light.
S2 Heavy wood floats.
I Heavy wood floats. Okay.
S2 Two things that float. Only one contains air.
S2 So it can't be that.
I And number three ... ?
S2 It's got to be number three ... by a process of elimination.

Inconsistent use of evidence
In some cases, the students used only parts of the evidence presented, some showed inconsistencies in their reasoning and a few students made no reference to the evidence at all in their choice of explanation. Some, especially older students, chose an explanation because they 'knew' it to be 'correct', as in the following example relating to electric circuits:

S Number three.
I Can you tell me why?
S Well we reasoned that if it were number two and it was flowing both ways that one would be ... well, from our knowledge we know that it can't flow both ways!
I Okay. Right. What about the other ones then? One and four?
S That one [Explanation 4], it says it doesn't use anything up, but the batteries eventually go flat.

('Electric circuits'; age 16)

Relating new evidence to a chosen explanation

This part of the probe required students to use their chosen explanation to interpret new evidence. In the 'Electric circuits' context, four new circuits were presented in succession. The students were first asked to predict what would happen in each new situation. It was noticeable that many students made their predictions on the basis of existing knowledge and experience, rather than by applying their chosen explanation to this new situation. Rather than using the chosen explanation, whether theory or generalization, to predict, they used it retrospectively to justify and elaborate on their expected outcome. Of those who did make predictions, some used valid reasoning from their chosen theory or generalization.

When the outcome of each new situation was demonstrated, the students were asked to comment on how their prediction related to the observation. In some cases, the theory or generalization appeared to be understood in such a loose form that it could account for almost any outcome. This appears to be the case in the following example in which the students have selected explanation 2 (in which electricity goes along both wires from the battery to the bulb) and are asked to make predictions:

I   I add another bulb to this circuit . . . Using explanation number two, what do you think will happen when I connect up here? What will we see?

S1 Dimmer bulb.

S2 It electricity from one . . . from that end of the battery . . . it'd be joining there. It'd be joining somewhere . . .

I   So the electricity will be joining somewhere – in the middle of the wire, between the bulbs?

S1 It's if number two's right.

I   If number two's right. Okay. But both of the bulbs will still light. Is that right?

S1 Yeah.

I   Will they light the same as each other or different?

S1 Should be the same.

I   Right. So they'll be although it meets in the middle the fact that there's electricity going through each of these bulbs will make them light.

S1 Mm.

('Electric circuits'; aged 16)

In this example, the students did not make clear how their predictions (that both bulbs would light, but more dimly than a single bulb) followed from their chosen explanation. Some students made *ad hoc* modifications to, or contradicted aspects of, their chosen explanation. Most of the students were able to discuss their prediction in relation to their chosen explanation, but others could not, even when asked directly. In the 'Floating and sinking' context, new pieces of evidence were presented after the students had selected their explanation. Some students went back spontaneously to their chosen explanation and many were able to do so when asked. Some students, however, appeared to be prepared to accept different explanations to account for different examples in this context.

Overall, similarities were noted in both contexts in the ways students related pieces of evidence to explanation (either theory or generalization). Where evidence was in agreement with prediction from the students' theory or generalization, this was normally recognized as such. As we have already noted, however, for some students, the theory or generalization appeared to be used in such a loose form that any new evidence could be accommodated. In some situations where the evidence was in agreement with the prediction from the theory or generalization, valid deductions from the theory or generalization were made; in others, *ad hoc* modifications were made to the theory or generalization to accommodate aspects of the new evidence.

When evidence was perceived as conflicting with the chosen theory or generalization, this led to an expression of dissatisfaction with the explanation chosen, *ad hoc* modification of the explanation chosen, rejection of the evidence, or (with some younger students) retention of the explanation despite its mismatch with the evidence. It is of interest to note the considerable agreement between this list and the forms of response to anomalous data reported by Chinn and Brewer (1993).

General features of coordination of evidence and explanation

A number of types of features appeared to be drawn upon by students in responding to all aspects of this probe, whether selecting explanations, using them to make predictions or coordinating particular pieces of evidence with selected explanations. These features include the ways in which empirical evidence was drawn upon, the use made of knowledge of the phenomenon in question, and the conceptual ideas that students had about the explanations offered in justifying their responses.

The students' responses were classified into five groups, according to the ways in which empirical evidence, familiarity with the phenomena in question, and conceptual ideas about the explanations offered were used in discussing and justifying responses. The five categories are:

1 *Consistent use of evidence and explanation.* Responses in which available evidence had been used consistently in all parts of the explanation.
2 *Inconsistent use of evidence and explanation.* Responses in which there was inconsistency between all or parts of the available evidence and the explanation.
3 *Phenomenon-based reasoning.* Responses based on a familiarity with the behaviour of the phenomena (either electric circuits or objects floating and sinking) rather than based on the chosen explanation or evidence presented.
4 *Prior 'knowledge' of explanation.* Responses based on the students' declared knowledge of the domain rather than on the explanations or evidence presented. This declared knowledge may or may not be correct.
5 *Other.* Responses which could not be classified into the above four categories.

When analysed in terms of these categories, a consistent pattern of age-related differences in students' responses emerged. The results are shown in Fig. 7.7. There was a noticeable and statistically significant difference with age in the number of responses involving consistent use of evidence and explanation as compared with all other types of response ($p < 0.05$, χ^2). There was also a decreasing trend with age in inconsistencies in reasoning and in the use of phenomenon-based reasoning. A number of other specific age-related features were noted in the students' responses. Some younger students appeared not to differentiate between evidence and explanation in selecting explanations. This was less apparent, however, in their use of evidence to evaluate explanations. Older students were also more likely to appreciate that explanations can be evaluated empirically, independently of their belief or disbelief in the explanation.

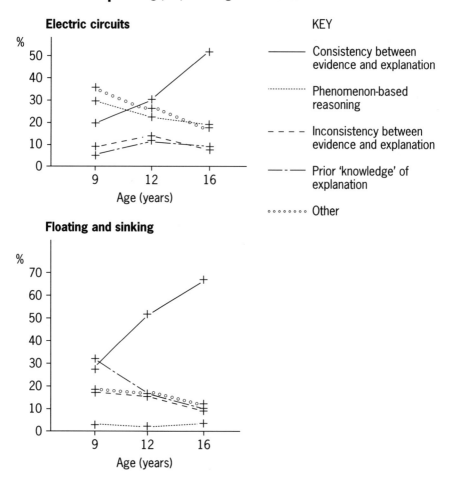

Figure 7.7 Prevalence of different responses to the coordination of evidence and explanation.

Our general conclusions from the results of this probe are that the majority of students of all ages made some attempt to evaluate explanations with the evidence presented, thus giving support to the view that they can distinguish between evidence and explanation. The results for the youngest students, however, need to be interpreted with caution, as in some cases their understanding of the explanations presented was tenuous. Furthermore, it appeared that, especially with the youngest students, no distinction tended to be made between the status of a given explanation and evidence: both were seen as presented 'facts'. It appears that the consistent coordination of evidence and explanation increases with age and that by age 16 most students not only distinguish between evidence and explanation, but also appear to be able to evaluate explanations presented in the light of evidence. In some cases, this occurs even when students state explicitly their disbelief in the explanations. The finding that the majority of students at age 16 are capable of coordinating evidence and explanation in this way does not by itself indicate that students appreciate the centrality of this kind of reasoning in science.

| Summary

This chapter has presented evidence, from a number of probes, about young people's views on the nature, status and validation of scientific knowledge. We have seen how, at the simplest level, scientific knowledge is portrayed as a picture of events in the world with little distinction being made between evidence and explanations. The most sophisticated portrayal, on the other hand, is of scientific knowledge as a theoretical model of events, a model which can be evaluated in the light of evidence. As a result of the data and analysis presented in both this and the previous chapter, we have elaborated a general framework to characterize dimensions of students' epistemological reasoning. This is presented and discussed in Chapter 8.

8 | A framework for characterizing features of students' epistemological reasoning in science

In Chapter 7, we developed a portrayal of students' views of the nature and status of scientific knowledge by characterizing their responses to a number of probes. Our account focused on three strands of this epistemological dimension in students' representations of science: what young people see as characterizing scientific enquiry; their views on the nature and status of scientific theories; and the relationship between theories and evidence. In our analysis, we noticed some common features of students' reasoning occurring across the different probes. This suggested to us that it might be possible to generate a general framework to describe major features of students' epistemological representations.

The framework that we propose is summarized in Table 8.1. This framework is the result of both theoretical analysis and empirical enquiry. We have drawn on the literature relating to the nature of scientific knowledge to help us identify epistemological features of relevance. We have then compared the types of reasoning that the students used in response to different probes in order to characterize the different representations apparent within each feature. The framework which we propose is a general typology of the distinct ways in which the **nature and status of scientific knowledge** is represented in students' discourse. It does not describe patterns in reasoning by individual students.

| The framework

The proposed framework identifies three qualitatively distinct epistemological representations which we call *Phenomenon-based reasoning, Relation-*

Table 8.1 A framework for characterizing features of students' epistemological representations.

Form of reasoning	Form of scientific enquiry	Nature of explanation	Relationship between explanation and description
Phenomenon-based reasoning	**Focus on phenomenon** • Enquiry as observation of the behaviour of phenomenon, i.e. 'Look and see' • Making phenomena happen so that consequent behaviour can be observed	**Explanation as description** • Description of phenomenon; no distinction between description and explanation	**No distinction** • No clear separation between description of phenomenon and explanation
Relation-based reasoning	**Correlating variables** • Interventions in, or planned observations of, the behaviour of phenomena are needed to find explanations. These involve: – controlled intervention in phenomena, such as fair testing – identification of influential variables – outcomes related to conditions	**Empirical generalization** • Explanation as relation between features of phenomenon which are observable/taken as existing (e.g. heat, vacuum). Such relationships can take the form of: – correlation between variables – linear causal sequence • Alternative possible variables may be entertained. However, only one relationship assumed to be true. Additional or alternative factors which might influence the situation may not be considered. As a consequence, correlation tends to be interpreted as causal	**Inductive relationship** • Recognition that description and explanation are distinct, but both use the same language categories, i.e. refer to features which are observable/taken as existing • Explanation is seen as emerging from data; is expressed in same language categories as data and expresses the relationship between taken-for-granted features of the situation • The relation between theory and evidence is seen as unproblematic; theories can be 'proved'

Table 8.1 *cont.*

Form of reasoning	Form of scientific enquiry	Nature of explanation	Relationship between explanation and description
Model-based reasoning	Evaluate theory • Enquiry can involve evaluation of theory or model in the light of evidence • The relationship between theoretical knowledge and natural phenomenon is acknowledged as being problematic	Modelling • Theories and models are conjectural • Explanation as involving coherent stories involving posited theoretical entities • Explanation involves discontinuity between observation and theoretical entities • Multiple possible models are entertained	Hypothetico-deductive • Clear distinction made between description and explanation • Recognition that proposing an explanation involves conjectures about theoretical entities of a different category to the observed or taken-for-granted features of the situation • Explanation cannot be logically deduced from observational data • Recognition of the provisional status of theories; can never be certain that a theory is correct

based reasoning and *Model-based reasoning*. Each of these representations is associated with a distinctive way of portraying (1) scientific enquiry, (2) views of the nature of scientific explanation and (3) the relationship between explanation and description.

Phenomenon-based reasoning

The central feature of this representation is the lack of distinction which is made between description and explanation of phenomena. Scientific enquiry is portrayed as either direct observation of phenomena ('you look and see') or as an intervention in a phenomenon in order to 'try it and see what happens'. Explanation is seen as a redescription of the phenomenon and, as such, it is seen as an unproblematic portrayal of 'how things are'. For example, the student who commented that scientists can find answers to the question 'Is the Earth's atmosphere heating up?' by 'sending people outside the Earth to see', is reasoning in this way. Enquiry here is seen as providing direct access to knowledge of the world as it is. In discussing the 'Germs' story, a 16-year-old commented that you could be sure that milk goes off because microbes grow better when it's warm, because 'When you put them in the fridge it doesn't get rid of them. It just . . . they don't grow as quickly'. This representation also portrays explanation as a taken-for-granted statement of how the world is, with no distinction being made between explanation and evidence.

Relation-based reasoning

In this representation, a distinction is made between evidence and explanation. Explanations take the form of empirical generalizations; in other words, they are relations between observable features, or features which are taken-for-granted as existing in the material world and are described in the same language categories as observations.

In some cases, such empirical generalizations take the form of correlations between variables, for example, 'the larger the crystals, the slower they dissolve'. In other cases, they take the form of a chain of cause-and-effect relationships or linear causal reasoning. In such cases, intermediate agents with material properties are often postulated, for example, 'the heat makes the air rise and the air move up and makes the balloon fill up'. Here, heat is seen as a quasi-material agent acting on the air.

There is limited scope for conjecture within this representation. Although alternative possible factors may be entertained in developing empirical generalizations, there is a tendency to assume that one of these will be true and that the explanation is in a correspondence relationship with the material world. This may be due to a confusion between correlational reasoning and linear causal reasoning. The result is that, in cases of correlational reasoning, students tend to consider only one factor as possibly influencing the situation – the one which they see as the 'cause'. As a consequence, other possible influential factors are overlooked.

A further feature of this view of explanation is that it is seen to emerge from data in an inductive way. Empirical investigations of such generalizations involve 'proving' that the stated variables do, in fact, influence the phenomenon in question (for example, that salt speeds up the rusting process), without any reference to underlying mechanisms. Enquiry thus involves determining relationships between identifiable features or variables in describing the behaviour of phenomena. Designed interventions or planned observations are needed to do this. Such interventions involve identifying possible influential variables, conducting controlled experiments and relating outcomes to initial conditions.

Model-based reasoning

The core feature of this representation is explanatory modelling. Explanations, rather than being grounded in the language of observations, are expressed in terms of a different theoretical system. So, for example, the behaviour of a gas-filled balloon when heated is 'explained' in terms of the properties of posited entities such as air molecules. The macroscopic system is modelled in terms of the behaviour of a microscopic 'ensemble' of particles.

Scientific enquiry, from this point of view, involves the evaluation of conjectured models in the light of evidence. It is recognized that empirical evidence can never 'prove' the truth of a conjectured model, although it can eliminate competing conjectures. Theories, therefore, have a provisional status.

An important feature of theories or explanations in this case is that they are expressed in a different language from the language of observations; the language used describes the behaviour of the theoretical entities posited (whether molecules, electric fields or genetic code) within a theoretical system. Explanations thus involve coherent 'stories' involving posited theoretical entities and there is thus a discontinuity between observations and explanations. Furthermore, since theories are conjectural, more than one is, in principle, possible.

A clear distinction is thus made between description and explanation within this form of representation. A description is given in terms of a language relating to the observed phenomena; the explanation is given in terms of a language which describes the behaviour of the conjectured model. From this point of view, therefore, theories or explanations cannot be deduced directly from observational data. A creative act is necessary to produce a theory or model. The consistency of the observations with the conjectured model can then be evaluated. In our analysis of students' responses to the various probes, we only saw evidence of parts of this *Model-based reasoning*. Some aspects were weakly represented or not portrayed at all. Such aspects include the recognition of the provisional status of theories and the possibility of entertaining alternative theoretical models. We include all these aspects in our framework, however, for the sake of completeness.

| Interpretation of the framework

It is important to emphasize that the proposed framework is a typology of the representations of epistemological reasoning found in the discourse of the sample as a whole. As such, it is an attempt to characterize features in the scientific reasoning of school students and to summarize these in a way which may be useful to those people, including science teachers, who are interested in the communication of science.

As we indicated earlier, the framework does not aim to portray reasoning at an individual level. The fact that a student is identified as using *Model-based reasoning* in one situation implies nothing about the form of reasoning which that student may use in a different situation. First, our enquiry was not designed to investigate claims about student reasoning at an individual level. Second, it may be completely appropriate for different representations to be used in different contexts in science.

A further point about the framework which requires clarification is whether or not it represents a hierarchy in forms of representation. At a theoretical level, it does represent a hierarchy in terms of the complexity of the reasoning involved. However, in specific situations in science, it is quite possible that any one of the three forms of reasoning may be the most appropriate to use. We are not, therefore, claiming that *Model-based reasoning* is necessarily better than *Relation-based reasoning*. Different situations may demand different representations. A further related point concerns whether the framework represents a development sequence. Although a longitudinal study would be necessary to confirm this, this study enables us to make some comments on this issue. Overall, *Phenomenon-based reasoning* tended to be used most, but not exclusively, by the youngest age group. *Relation-based reasoning* was the most common representation among 12- and 16-year-olds, although there was some variation across situations. The prevalence of *Model-based reasoning* was seen to increase with age. However, it was still a minority of students whose responses reflected this representation by age 16, and certain features of the representation, such as an awareness of the conjectural nature of theories and their provisional status, were represented in the responses of one or two students only.

We suggest from this that most school students have not been called upon to use *Model-based reasoning* explicitly. This may inhibit their understanding of some scientific situations where modelling is required and make it difficult for them to respond appropriately.

Here we are not saying that students are *not able* to use *Model-based reasoning*, but that, in situations where such reasoning would have been appropriate, that they *did not* use it. The reason why this occurred, of course, may be a consequence of the tasks we asked them to do. It can also can be interpreted either in terms of personal cognitive development of the students, in terms of the portrayal of science in school science lessons or some interaction between the two. This is an issue which will be considered further in the final chapter.

9 | Students' views of science as a social enterprise

| Introduction

This chapter addresses the third of the key features of interest in this research study, namely, students' understandings of science as a social enterprise. As we indicated in Chapter 5, we see this feature as including students' ideas about both the internal workings of the scientific community itself and the external relations of science with society. In order to elicit students' views on such complex matters, we thought it was important to set any discussions within clearly specified contexts. The most appropriate contexts, it seemed to us, would be cases where there is dispute in the scientific community, as in such cases the social relations and interactions within the scientific community become more clearly apparent. We therefore chose two cases as a basis for our probe **Closure of Debates**, both of which are examples of scientific controversies: one, the dispute surrounding Wegener's theory of continental drift, is internal to science; the other, the dispute about the safety of food irradiation, concerns a particular application of science in society.

| Science as a social enterprise

Science does not exist in a social and cultural 'vacuum'. Rather, it impinges on society in a variety of ways, influencing it profoundly and in turn being influenced by it. Most obviously, the technological products of scientific understanding have a major effect on our daily lives. Much of this has become taken-for-granted as part of the fabric of ordinary existence. The influence of science, however, is not simply material; scientific knowledge and methods of enquiry colour our view of the world and of ourselves. Midgley (1992: 1) comments that:

> Any system of thought playing the huge part that science now plays in our lives must also shape our guiding myths and colour our imaginations profoundly. It is not just a useful tool. It is also a pattern that we follow at a deep level in trying to meet our imaginative needs.

We become particularly aware of the impact of science and technology on our lives when there is dispute about a specific issue, such as the purity of water supplies, the disposal of nuclear waste, the consequences of carbon dioxide emissions into the atmosphere, or the uses of knowledge of the human genome.

Conversely, society influences science. Interest groups of various sorts influence the directions of scientific work by funding some areas and not others. Individual scientists are also members of society, with a diverse set of views, opinions and values which derive from their wider commitments and interests. These may influence their decisions about the direction of their own work and may even, some have claimed, affect their interpretations of the natural world and hence scientific knowledge itself (see, for example, Mackenzie 1978; Freudenthal 1986; Longino 1990).

Science is itself, of course, a social enterprise. Scientific work is carried out by research groups, each linked into a larger network sharing a common interest in an area of enquiry, and in turn identifying with a particular scientific specialism. Well-established procedures regulate the sharing of information, through conferences and journals, with processes of peer review controlling the mechanisms by which the findings of individuals become transformed into public knowledge. (For a fuller discussion of the social processes within the scientific community, see Ziman 1967, 1978.)

In Chapter 2, we noted that an understanding of the relationship between science and the wider society, and of the internal social processes and relationships within the scientific community, has come to be seen as part of what might be meant by 'an understanding of science' – alongside some substantive scientific knowledge and an understanding of the scientific approach to enquiry. In this chapter, we focus on students' understanding of this social dimension of science. Chapter 2 reviewed the reasons why it might be thought important for young people (and for adults) to appreciate these social processes. Perhaps the most important argument concerns the resources which people may draw upon to interpret cases of dispute and disagreement about matters concerning science. Collins and Shapin (1986) have argued that an image of science as reliable knowledge, obtained through standard methods of enquiry, leaves people with little alternative, when faced with a dispute between scientists about some practical matter, but to attribute this to the bias or incompetence of one or both parties. An understanding of the social processes by which knowledge is negotiated and the validity and interpretation of data agreed would, they suggest, provide people with a better basis for understanding disagreement and reaching a view about what should, or should not, be done.

| Scientific disputes and their resolution

Scientific disputes not only bring the science–society relationship into sharp relief, but also provide a useful context for enquiry. They expose, in a particularly clear way, issues about the role of evidence and of social factors in shaping the course of a dispute and in determining the time and manner of its resolution. Aspects of the way that science as public knowledge is established, which are hidden from view during phases of 'normal science', become more readily apparent. Many recent studies of science by historians, philosophers and sociologists have focused on such disputes and their eventual resolution (see, for example, Barnes and Shapin 1979; Collins 1981a; Pickering 1984). Collins (1975: 205–206) notes a particular advantage of studies of current scientific developments:

> when we consider the grounds of knowledge, we do it within an environment filled with objects of knowledge which are already established. To speak figuratively, it is as though epistemologists are concerned with the characteristics of ships (knowledge) in bottles (validity) while living in a world where all ships are already in bottles with the glue dried and the strings cut. A ship within a bottle is a natural object in this world, and because there is no way to reverse the process, it is not easy to accept that the ship was ever a bundle of sticks ... My contention is that ... it is possible to make a partial escape from the cultural determinism of current knowledge ... by looking at [facts and ideas] while they are being formed, before they have become 'set' as part of anyone's natural (scientific) world. In short, the contemporaneous study of contemporary scientific developments ... can provide an entry.

As contexts for exploring students' views of the social dimension of science, however, studies of current science can have one substantial disadvantage: the science content and processes involved are often advanced and difficult. Historical controversies offer contexts for exploring the development of more accessible scientific knowledge. The use of historical materials in school science is not, however, without its attendant problems. Some knowledge of the background to the historical case is necessary if an understanding of the issues involved is to be more than superficial. Often this may involve the learning of scientific ideas which are no longer accepted. And it is difficult to prevent theory change coming to seem like the triumph of virtue over prejudice, to take seriously the perspective of those who 'lost' the argument. Despite these difficulties, there has been a recurrent strand within science curriculum writings of advocacy of a historical dimension in school science (Russell 1981; Matthews 1994), often supported by specimen teaching materials (Klopfer 1964; Rutherford *et al.* 1970; Aikenhead and Fleming 1975; Solomon 1989).

For the purposes of our research, scientific disputes also provided fruitful contexts, for reasons similar to those which have attracted historians and sociologists. Our principal interest was in the ideas students have about the social dimension of science. The resources students draw upon in discussing the reasons for disagreement between scientists and the ways in which agreement had been, or might be, reached provide insights into their awareness and understanding of this social dimension. Ideally, we would have liked to ask the students directly about these issues. But we could not be sufficiently confident that they had the necessary background information about any particular historical or current dispute to support an informed discussion about its causes or its resolution. So it seemed essential to provide this background, as quickly and efficiently as possible, to ensure that all the students involved had an adequate knowledge of the cases themselves before probing their interpretations of the dispute.

We tried out a number of contexts with students aged 9, 12 and 16 years and quickly came to the view that only the 16-year-olds were able to engage with the issues we were interested in. This may, of course, be because we failed to find suitable contexts to engage the younger students. In any event, we decided to explore these issues with the 16-year-olds only. From the contexts we tried, we selected two quite different ones for the main study: the controversy in the 1920s within the geology community about Alfred Wegener's hypothesis of continental drift, and the more recent (and still unresolved) issue in the UK about allowing the more general use of food irradiation. The historical case study explores students' ideas about issues internal to science, concerning the processes by which the scientific community reaches consensus about phenomena and their explanation. The contemporary case study probes students' ideas about the external social relations of science, and the processes by which society reaches a practical decision about an issue involving scientific knowledge.

For both case studies, teaching materials were specially prepared to provide the necessary background information. These consisted of an audiotape and an accompanying booklet. The students followed the booklet, under direction from the audiotape. This took about 30 minutes and included some exercises to ensure the students' engagement with the material. Then, in groups of four, the students were asked to discuss some questions about the reasons for the disagreement between scientists, and about how it might be resolved. A researcher then joined each group and asked the students to explain their thinking about each of the questions in turn, probing answers for clarification or to explore issues more deeply. The group discussions, both with and without the researcher present, were tape-recorded and transcribed.

Twelve such groups were interviewed about each of the two cases. These were drawn from classes in two comprehensive schools, one with a predominantly working-class and the other a predominantly middle-class catchment area. The transcripts were analysed to document the different arguments used by the student groups in tackling each question, and then to identify similarities and patterns in these arguments, leading to an overview of the students' reasoning about these issues.

The research questions which our analysis focused on included:

> Do students see the scientific enterprise as a social (as opposed to an individual) endeavour?
>
> How do students interpret conflicts within the scientific community? How do they see these being resolved?
>
> What do students see as the influence of society at large on the generation of scientific knowledge and on the application of that knowledge in specific contexts?

The case of Wegener and continental drift

The issue

In 1915, a German meteorologist, Alfred Wegener, published a book entitled *Die Entstehung der Kontinente und Ozeane (The Origin of the Continents and Oceans)*, in which he set out his view that the continents have drifted apart and are fragments of an original 'super-continent'. The English version of the book appeared in 1922. In that same year, the British Association for the Advancement of Science held a meeting to discuss the drift hypothesis; a similar symposium was held in 1925 by the American Association of Petroleum Geologists, with Wegener present. Both meetings gave a largely hostile response to Wegener's ideas; the notion of drift was rejected by the geological community. Over the following three decades, however, further evidence of continental drift was collected from a variety of sources, culminating in the work of Vine and Matthews in the early 1960s on magnetic anomalies around sea-floor ridges which led to the notion of sea-floor spreading. By the end of the 1960s, the theory of plate tectonics involving the drift of continents in the way Wegener had proposed had become the widely accepted orthodoxy among geologists and Earth scientists.

The history of the drift hypothesis is a good story in its own right and several accessible popular accounts exist (Tarling and Tarling 1971; Hallam 1975). It has also been used widely as a case study to explore and test ideas about the dynamics of scientific theory change. Some have seen the episode as closely matching Lakatos's views about theory change (Frankel 1979); others have explored its match with the Kuhnian notion of revolution and paradigm change (Jones 1974; Kitts 1974). LeGrand (1988) provides a detailed account of the history of the continental drift hypothesis with an accompanying philosophical 'commentary'. The Wegener case has also been used as a vehicle for teaching ideas about the nature of scientific enquiry at the tertiary level (Open University 1981) and to illustrate ideas about the role of theory in school science education (Duschl 1990).

Providing background information

Students were presented with background information about the Wegener controversy as we have described above. This concluded with a series of cartoons which presented some of the main arguments for and against Wegener's idea of continental drift. The students were then asked to work in groups of four, to discuss the following questions:

- Why do you think the geologists in the 1920s did not all agree?
- What do you think would have been needed in the 1920s to enable all the geologists to reach agreement?
- Why do you think the majority of geologists in the 1920s reached a decision which we now think is the wrong one?

All three questions raised similar issues and discussion moved fluidly between them. Some possible answers were, of course, suggested in the presentation of background information, but it was then of interest to see how the students selected from these and expressed the ideas they chose to use in their own words.

Students' reasoning

The students' ideas about the reasons for disagreement between scientists about continental drift and about how it might have been resolved fell into two broad categories: (1) *empirical* explanations, based on ideas about the quantity, quality or nature of the available evidence; and (2) *social* explanations, based on ideas about the likely behaviour of individuals or groups. All student groups, in the course of discussion, offered explanations of both kinds. The two categories are not entirely distinct, with empirical arguments often used to provide a rationale for certain types of social action. There were also interesting variants of view and of emphasis within each category.

Empirical explanations of disagreement and its resolution

All twelve groups of students interviewed used arguments about the quantity, quality or nature of the evidence available to geologists in the 1920s to explain the disagreement between them. Several groups argued that the rejection of Wegener's ideas in the 1920s was primarily due to the lack of sufficient evidence. Eleven of the twelve groups also argued that the *quality* of the available evidence was significant, and put improvements in the quality of evidence down to the availability of better equipment:

S   They needed more equipment and stuff won't they?

S   They didn't have the gear did they?

S   They didn't have the technology we do now, so we can make better decisions ... they weren't as accurate as we can get them now, and they were saying all the rock were a perfect fit. They could have been wrong ...

Underlying many of these discussions of 'better evidence' from improved 'technology' or 'equipment' is the idea of the sure, or certain, fact. For one group, disagreement arose 'because they didn't have sufficient proof or solid facts'.

Many groups appeared to believe that really convincing evidence would be *direct* rather than indirect. We have already seen this emphasis on direct evidence in responses to other probes in the study, notably the **Warrants for Belief** probe (Chapter 7). One student commented that 'You can't see the movement ... you can't prove it'; as a result, scientists did not have '100% proof either way'. Ten of the twelve groups mentioned direct measurements of the movement of continents as the evidence needed to resolve disagreements and reach consensus. Satellites and lasers were seen as tools which made such measurements possible.

S   All their evidence, it wasn't rock solid [laughs].

I   What kind of evidence would have been rock solid? What kinds of things would convince someone?

S   Accurate measurements.

S   The ground moving.

S   See that it's moving.

S   ... they didn't have satellite pictures that they couldn't see how it was changing.

S   They couldn't measure it.

S   If you could put a laser from a mountain over here and a mountain over there and see if you could attach it to the other side and see the amount of time it takes it from getting from one to the other ... Maybe they'd be able to see if they were moving back.

Interpretation of evidence

Several groups became involved in discussions about interpretations of the evidence. One student explained his rejection of the 'land bridge' idea in terms of its failure to account for coastline fitting:

S   I believe it was land there one time that joined them.

S   Yeah, but then you wouldn't get the shapes that Wegener ... that would be absolute fluke that you'd get the same shapes.

Another student argued that there might be reasons other than continental drift to explain the locations of coal deposits:

S Well, they'd say like that there were different temperatures all around the world. Two points could be the same with tropical trees growing.

Reasoning of this sort indicates an ability to consider evidence and theory as separate entities, using the former to test the latter. For many, however, in Collins' metaphor, the ship (of knowledge) seemed to be securely inside its bottle, and evidence and explanation were closely bound up with each other, making alternative accounts difficult to entertain:

I   So do you think the theory that the continents were once stuck together is sensible?
S   Yes.
S   Yes.
I   Why?
S   Because we know. Because we have that Wegener bloke...
S   So many textbooks have said that this is right.

The absence of any mechanism for continental drift is often seen as an important reason for the rejection of drift ideas in the 1920s. The proposal of such a mechanism in the 1930s, based on circulating convection currents in the Earth's mantle driven by the heating effect of radioactive decay processes, was a significant link in the chain of events leading to the eventual acceptance of the drift hypothesis in the 1960s. This idea, however, appeared surprisingly infrequently in students' discussions. As the idea of absence of a mechanism was included in the introductory material as an aspect of the dispute, its absence from most groups' discussion is noteworthy.

Social accounts of disagreement and its resolution

All twelve student groups also provided social accounts of the disagreement between scientists. For several groups, disagreement was 'natural', a common, even desirable, feature of social life:

I Do you expect scientists to have arguments?
S Yes.
I Why?
S They've all got different ideas haven't they? People have different ideas. They're still going to have arguments.

S People think differently don't they. They have different views with everything, really isn't it?
S No-one ever agrees with something, with the same thing.
S People argue with you 'cause, if everybody agreed you'd be a bit boring. We'd be wearing the same thing and doing the same thing in the same way.

One explanation offered for a lack of consensus was that different individuals or groups had access to different pieces of evidence. Several groups argued that poorer communications in the 1920s, and the fact that travel was slower and more difficult, would account for differences of view:

> S Because different geologists collected different information and they like based their theories on the information that they had collected, and seeing as different men had different information therefore their theory would have been different.
> S Because they were all working on different information. If they'd all had each other's information. . . .
> S . . . they might come up with a similar idea.

No group, however, went on from this apparent acceptance of the 'naturalness' of disagreement between people to note that science, at school level, is marked by consensus rather than dispute, and to attempt to reconcile this apparent anomaly.

Several groups mentioned the tendency of people, including scientists, to stick to ideas with which they are familiar.

> S They were used to that way of thinking and they didn't want to change their minds. They wanted to believe in what they were on about.
> S They were just intent on believing what they'd decided on and they didn't want to listen to anybody else who told them that they were wrong.

A few groups tried to justify this rejection of new ideas, suggesting that novel ideas, proposed by someone with no background in the area, are likely to be rejected:

> S They thought Wegener was a waste of time.
> I But most of the evidence you said convinced *you*. They did have evidence.
> S But they were stuck in their own ways weren't they?
> S Yeah, 'cause they'd been working all their lives really hadn't they to find something. Then this one person pops up and says all the countries and continents have been joined together.

One student linked the commitment to existing ideas to her own experiences of classroom debates:

> S Some people might end up even if they don't believe they might be arguing. I know in like geography when we've done things before people like in the group they all say, 'We're right because it's our theory, and no-one else is right'. I've seen it sometimes when we've had discussions it goes over the top.

Another group noted that the adoption of a new idea could take time, echoing Planck's observation that 'a new scientific truth does not triumph by convincing its opponents and making them see the light, but rather because its opponents eventually die, and a new generation grows up that is familiar with it' (Planck 1949, cited in Kuhn 1970: 151):

S There's hardly any evidence to tell us.
I And do you think that if we had better technology that we would all agree?
S Oh no, because . . . you can't get someone to agree, but maybe you can get their sons or daughters to agree and then gradually it gets accepted that way.
S . . . It takes a while to be accepted.

Finally, several groups acknowledged the commitment of time and effort which scientists had invested in their previous work and careers, and identified this as a reason for reluctance to accept novel ideas:

S Because they'd all been doing geology all their lives and they didn't want to change it all.
S Yeah. They've all be doing work like this and then this Wegener person just popped up and gets all the ideas.
S It should mean all their work was wrong.

That Wegener was a meteorologist, not a geologist, was pointed out in the introductory material presented to the students. Half of the groups made reference to this idea in accounting for the reception of Wegener's ideas.

S Well, you'd be a bit wary of his theory.
S It came out all of a sudden.
S He's got all these big theories. It's hard to believe at first.
S He's not even a geologist.

S . . . you know like rivalry . . . because he's like not one of them. Like an outsider coming in and like butting in on them.
S He didn't understand it enough. He just basically . . . He knew about the weather. That's all they thought, but he actually wanted to know about other things as well.

This idea of personal rivalries was not mentioned in the background material but arose in the discussions of almost half of the groups. Interestingly, several groups indicated that they felt such rivalries were much less likely in contemporary science than they had been in the 1920s. In part, this was attributed to the availability of better technology, and hence more accurate measurements, leading to the quicker and more effective resolution of disputes.

Students' reasoning: a summary

Most students, in responding to the Wegener case study, saw evidence as the key factor leading to consensus. Failure to agree is due to shortage of evidence, or to unreliable evidence. The shortcomings in available evidence permit social factors to operate, and factions to argue their case success-fully. Better communication and, above all, better (and preferably direct) evidence will, in the eyes of the great majority of these students, cut through partisan commitments. There is widespread confidence that em-pirical evidence can unproblematically resolve issues of theory choice, and reveal 'how the world is'. The students' separation of theory and evidence is perhaps less clear than we might ideally have wished, and the idea that evidence provides raw material for judging and evaluating theory, rather than giving unproblematic access to the 'truth', seems not to be widely held, or well developed.

The case of the safety of food irradiation

Background to the problem

Food irradiation involves the bombardment of food with gamma radia-tion. The process kills bacteria and other microorganisms which can carry disease and slows down the ripening process, giving produce such as fruit and vegetables a longer shelf-life.

Research into the safety of food irradiation has been carried out in many countries. Studies have been funded by the United Nations Food and Agricultural Organization and the International Atomic Energy Agency. These bodies set up a joint Expert Committee on Food Irradiation, which has recommended limits on food irradiation doses. Following these inter-nationally established guidelines, a number of countries now permit irra-diation of selected items of food. In the UK, however, concerns have been expressed about the safety of the process. Critics point to research that indicates that irradiation of food can produce an increase in free radicals which may be implicated in producing genetic changes and cancers. To date, the use of food irradiation in the UK is not allowed by law except in cases where patients in hospitals may have their food irradiated to minimize the risk of infection.

Background information provided to the students

The students were presented with background information about the pro-cess of food irradiation using an audiotape and booklet as described earlier in the chapter. The background information included a description of a food irradiation plant. The effect of gamma radiation of foods was then outlined. A table of permitted doses used in the Netherlands was presented in the booklet. The issues involved in the controversy were introduced through a newspaper cutting which reported a debate in the House of Com-mons in 1990. The points for and against food irradiation were then pre-sented in a dialogue between two scientists, one from a university food science department and the other from a food industries research department. In the dialogue, evidence from a range of studies was presented and discussed, and a number of arguments both for and against food irradiation were considered.

After reviewing the information presented in the booklet, the students were asked to discuss why two research scientists should disagree. In order to guide their discussion, they were asked to consider and discuss three possible reasons and then to come to a view about which of these they agreed with. The three reasons were:

- They do not have all the facts. Once you have all the facts, then an answer to the question would be clear.
- They have all the facts they need. No matter how many facts you have, you always have to make a judgement about what the facts mean.
- The scientist working for the food industry is influenced by what is profitable for the industry.

Students' reasoning

As with the previous case, the students' ideas about the reasons for disagreement between the scientists were seen to fall into two broad categories: (1) *empirical* explanations based on the nature of the available evidence and (2) *social* explanations based on their knowledge of the behaviour of individuals or groups.

Empirical explanations of disagreement

All the groups in the study used arguments about the quality, quantity or nature of the evidence available to account for the difference in opinion of the two scientists.

Lack of facts

The most common argument which the students advanced focused on the need for more facts. Two assumptions could be seen to be implicit in this view: first, truth was seen to emerge from the facts themselves; second, the notion of 'hard facts', facts which were unambiguous and incontrovertible in themselves, was dominant as the following extracts illustrate:

S If there was some hard facts that showed it was safe.

S I think actually if they did proper tests and they had more facts and they did it on a large group of people – they'd probably find out, wouldn't they.

S When you've found out definitely what it does and if it's dangerous.

S You can try and find out how much is actually dangerous.

S They can tell can't they. A fact's a fact.

The notion of a 'hard fact' as one which is quantified was also apparent:

S They've got some facts, but they are not very accurate are they? They did not come up with any figure or anything.

S They did not say like 80 per cent.

S No-one's mentioned any figures or anything, so they're not sure what they're talking about.

Interpretation of evidence

In most groups, proof was seen as emerging from the facts. Indeed, there were explicit references to needing to know 'all the facts':

S If they had more facts, they could make a better conclusion.

S A larger survey.

S They need to do some more to see if they can get any more proof. They should do it on a worldwide spread really, like people all over the world and nourished and undernourished people.

S They don't know all the facts. If they did they'd be able to reach a decision and see if it was dangerous or not.

There was a recognition, however, that knowing all the facts could be problematic. It could take time and resources.

S 'Cause I mean you can't tell about like long-term effects and they'll be different when you've got people, on like these genetic disorders, you're not going to find out for, you know, like generations and people are always going to be arguing about summat or other . . .

S It would take a long time to get the full facts. You'd have to use a lot of libraries and other people.

A minority of students recognized that certainty was impossible:

S There is no way you could get all the facts. And like, you can't test them on everyone, can you?

S It's like these genetic things and stuff like that. They're not going to come out for a long time are they? At the moment they haven't got any evidence that exists, but they could think . . . well we'll put all the facts that we possibly have, make it legal and support it and everything and five years later . . . oh . . . summat's happened. Like that drug they gave to pregnant women. And the women had deformed babies.

In some groups, the students recognized that judgements would need to be made. There's going to be no way of proving it. 'It won't be crystal clear, but it will be a lot easier to see.' One student, in all the discussions, indicated an awareness of a wider community of scientists being involved:

S An answer comes from a lot of investigation. You wouldn't need just one scientist. You'd need a load all from different backgrounds and stuff. It wouldn't just be one bloke. You'd need a lot of different people. A load of different facts from totally independent people.

Social accounts of disagreement

Social accounts for the disagreements between the scientists were also advanced by all the groups. In some cases, the students drew on their knowledge of human behaviour to explain the dispute. For example, they were aware of the possibility of bias, suggesting 'They're only using the facts that go with their argument'. As we saw in the case of the Wegener dispute, the students were also aware that scientists may be unwilling to change their position on an issue for personal reasons:

S They won't want to be proved wrong. If they are going round saying to everybody it [irradiated food] can't harm you, they don't want to look stupid by admitting they're wrong.

Social pressures were also readily identified as having an influence. For example, scientists working for a company were seen to be likely to take a biased view:

S He's bound to protect his own job.
S They're bound to go for whichever gets most money really.
S If they're saving millions with irradiation they're going to carry on with irradiation.

There was, however, evidence that the students had knowledge of checks and balances in society, as the following extract illustrates:

S He's going to be a bit cautious though – he could be sued if people die and stuff like that.

Students' reasoning: a summary

Overall, the students' discussions focused on bias or lack of facts as reasons for disagreements between scientists. The emerging picture is one of hard facts converging on firm conclusions, though there was evidence that some students recognized the problems associated with this view. The students certainly had a rich stock of knowledge about human nature and social institutions to use as a resource in thinking about these problems.

What was less well represented was a view of science in which theories are seen as conjectural and underdetermined by data, where measurements are seen as having inherent uncertainty, where scientific 'facts' are seen as products of a social as well as an empirical process, rather than a reading of nature.

| **Students' representations of the nature of scientific knowledge**

Epistemological aspects

What do these two case studies tell us about students' representations of the nature of science and scientific knowledge? Overall, the students' discussions focused more on lack of 'facts' or evidence, and on biases due to social or institutional positions or allegiances, than on inherent problems of interpretation of data. This in itself is not particularly surprising, as 'expert' accounts also discuss these aspects of most controversies at some length. It is, however, striking that, in both case studies, no student group explicitly argued that all the evidence available is (or was) indirect, and therefore open to different interpretations. Instead, we see a preoccupation with the quantity and quality of evidence but little inclination to stand back from the evidence and assess it *as a body of evidence*. Evidence seems to be regarded as 'information' or 'facts', which tell us 'how things are', rather than as raw material for conjecture about 'how things might be'. This is consistent with the impression gained from other probes that many students see explanations as 'emerging' from the data, rather than as a conjecture which might account for the data.

On the other hand, it seems clear that many 16-year-olds are aware that there is a problem in claiming that a piece of information is 'a fact' – unproblematically true. Many seem aware that facts can always be contested. Several groups also indicated by their comments an awareness that even possession of agreed 'facts' did not lead unproblematically to a single theory, and certainly did not 'prove' that the theoretical explanation was 'true'. In some cases, this seemed to lead towards a relativist interpretation of theory:

I What's the crucial information that makes us think a theory's correct? The main things?
S Because all the scientists believe it, we just believe what they say, so it could be that.

S We can't do anything.
S Prove that they [i.e. the continents] move?
S You can't do anything. It's based on a theory isn't it? I mean . . . nothing's proved in science. Like atoms and molecules and stuff. You can't definitely say that's true.
S You can't see them with a microscope. You can't see them.
S They just think this happens.

This apparent embracing of a relativist view corresponds to the stages of progression in accounting for beliefs proposed by Kitchener and King (1981; see also King *et al.* 1983). It could be that such a view is a necessary step in progression from a naive inductive view of natural knowledge towards a more sophisticated position. The overall picture of students' reasoning does, however, suggest that there are significant gaps in the 'bank' of resources available to them for accounting for disagreements about natural phenomena and events. This should not, we would suggest, necessarily be interpreted as a 'deficit model' of students' capabilities, but rather as raising questions about a curriculum which provides few opportunities for such issues to be raised and makes no attempt to develop ideas *about* science in an explicit or structured way.

Social processes

The **Closure of Debates** probe tends to corroborate the findings of other probes that students have little awareness of the role of internal and external social factors in the processes of developing and extending scientific knowledge. On the other hand, we see students making use of ideas from everyday life about disputes and their resolution to propose ways of resolving scientific controversies. Ordinary social experiences provide a rich source of raw material for constructing accounts based on ideas of bias, vested interest, rivalry, and so on. They also provide ideas about how disputes might be resolved.

Some students suggested that scientists who disagreed should both go to the same laboratory and do the experiment together – a joint test. Others suggested a form of adjudication. One group, for example, in discussing the Wegener case, argued that disputes would not easily be resolved by the groups involved; an independent arbitrator would be necessary to help them reach a resolution.

S What do you think they needed?
S Somebody in the middle. Someone that didn't have an opinion at all.
S Yeah, didn't favour one of them, or didn't favour the other.
S Somebody who were not biased on either side – to explain both sides.

This suggestion was also made in the case of 'Food irradiation'.

S You'd need a third person, wouldn't you, that's not even involved.
S There could be some blackmailing.
S You need a third party so they can't lie.
S So neither of them can lie. That third party's non-biased.

In one discussion, the adjudicator solution was suggested and, with charming innocence, a government minister was suggested as performing this function. Others used the legal process as their model for resolution of debates, and for exploring the notion of a 'fact':

S What I mean is, facts can be proved and disproved like theories can be proved and disproved, but I mean theoretically if everybody that had the correct facts, it probably could be proved. Yes. But people still try and disprove facts.

I So, what you're saying is no fact is really one hundred per cent absolutely certainly definitely true? Do you agree with that?

S I'm not sure really, 'cause like, well say like courts and stuff when they find like a court case, when they say this is a fact and you should be guilty of something. [It's not just] opinion, because they say their case is fact and if the facts are one hundred per cent right ... So they must be right, I think – the facts.

S You have to make up your own mind don't you? You don't know whether it's true or not [continental drift]. You have to make up your own mind.

I I see.

S It's up to you.

S It's like in court innit? You can't prove that somebody's guilty unless you know everything that happened.

S That's why they go away to court.

It seems clear, then, that students at this age can draw upon their experience of social interactions and can use their understanding of social interaction in general to account for actions in a scientific context. It seems equally clear that such ideas are frequently naive and superficial, and that some explicit curricular interventions are required if we wish to help students move towards a more subtle understanding of the nature of theory-making and theory-choice in science. The tools are available, but their deployment in sensitive and informed ways clearly requires more frequent and more carefully planned opportunities for practice and development.

| Summary

We noticed a striking similarity in features of the reasoning which students used in response to this probe and the characteristic responses given to the probes discussed in earlier chapters. For example, we see students emphasizing a view in which explanation in science is portrayed as emerging in an inductive way from data, rather than representing scientific explanation as conjectural and hence being underdetermined by data. This similarity is important from an educational point of view. It suggests that the features of the representations of scientific epistemology which we identified and discussed in Chapters 6 and 7, and summarized in the typology presented in Chapter 8, can also be identified in situations where students are considering authentic cases of contested science as in the case studies which were described in this chapter. This may be a strong indication, therefore, of the ways in which the representations of the nature of science portrayed in this study may be drawn on by students when they need to make decisions in their daily lives about science-related matters, especially in cases where uncertainty and differences of view exist.

If we see the ability to make sense of scientific controversies and disputes as an important facet of public understanding of science, then the findings of the **Closure of Debates** probe have implications for science curriculum planning. Several of these have been identified and discussed briefly in the course of this chapter. These will be considered further in the final chapter, where we will discuss the curriculum implications of the findings from this study.

10 | Young people's images of the nature of science: implications for science education

In this final chapter, we bring together the theoretical arguments for the place of teaching about the nature of science with the results from our research study on students' representations of science and consider the possible implications for science teaching in schools.

The case for teaching about the nature of science revisited

The arguments for teaching science and more particularly for teaching *about* science in the school curriculum were presented at length in Chapter 2. We now revisit these arguments in the light of the results of our survey and summarize what we see as the main reasons for including explicit teaching about the nature of science in science lessons.

Knowledge of the nature of science supports successful learning in science

We have argued that it is important for the successful learning of science for students to understand the nature of scientific knowledge itself. Although scientific work is carried out in a variety of ways, we would highlight the following as core features of scientific understanding: to appreciate that the purpose of science is to provide explanations for phenomena (and hence to distinguish it from technology); to understand that scientific explanation can take the form of theoretical conjecture (and does not emerge solely from observation); to appreciate that the basis for evaluation of such theories is through comparing predictions, derived from the theories, with observations of phenomena and that, to become accepted as part of the public knowledge of science, a new claim must be validated through the social processes of the scientific community. As we argued in Chapter 2, it is usual for the practices in science classrooms to portray a different view of scientific knowledge. It is common, for example, for students to be expected to draw conclusions from data as though such conclusions follow in a direct and logical way from observations. We are therefore not surprised that students are often confused about the status of conclusions drawn from classroom experiments given the way in which the epistemology of science tends to be represented in classrooms.

Knowledge of the nature of science contributes to more successful use of scientific knowledge in later life

It is a clearly stated goal of school science education that young people should be able to use the science knowledge that they acquire in school in the various facets of their future lives, whether as workers, parents, carers or as citizens.

As we argued earlier, the notion of applying scientific knowledge to new situations is not straightforward. In dealing with this problem of knowledge transfer, it is important that young people have an appreciation of the nature of scientific knowledge itself and are aware, for example, that the laws and theories of science are idealizations which may represent features of the behaviour of actual events or phenomena but may not account for all aspects of a complex situation. Understanding the applications of scientific knowledge, therefore, requires an appreciation of the way scientific explanations model the world.

Explanations differ in the degree to which we are confident or certain about them. Some explanations in science are so well grounded we no longer question them. However, it is recognized that this is not always the case, and it is therefore important that students appreciate the status of scientific explanations and are able to form judgements about the reliability and the limitations of the knowledge claims made by scientists. While much of the science that is taught in school is very well established and rarely contested (indeed, we would find it difficult to conceive of any other possible way of accounting for what we observe), there are many occasions in daily life when we find ourselves needing to make decisions, either as individuals or as members of public groups, based on knowledge which is less well grounded. The current public debates on the environmental effects of car emissions and the effect of specific foods on human health are illustrations of this. Halos of uncertainty also surround many scientific knowledge claims of social importance. Policy-makers and members of the public are being required to form judgements and to make decisions about such issues as greenhouse gases and global warming while recognizing that, for a range of reasons, science is not in a position to provide completely reliable knowledge. However, the fact that the knowledge that we have is uncertain and may even be contested does not mean that it is not worth taking into account – it is the best we have. Furthermore, it needs to be recognized that scientific knowledge itself may be only a component in a complex process of decision-making which can involve social, economic, ethical and political considerations.

Knowledge of the nature of science will enhance students' appreciation of science as a human endeavour

Teaching about the nature of science, and especially about the social, institutional and political frameworks within which science operates, can encourage students to see science as a human activity: a subject with a history, with its adventures and personalities, with big dramas and disputes. Through stories about the major developments in science, it is possible for students to appreciate the creative aspects of science, the place for ideas and speculation, as well as the disciplined job of checking them out. Such stories can also portray something of the ethical principles on which the scientific community attempts to base its work and the social processes through which science as public knowledge becomes established. If human beings, both as individual actors and as social groups, are put back into the teaching of science, then this may go some way to reducing the alienation from science that is increasingly being expressed by young people in our society.

| Students' views about the nature of science

To what extent are the perspectives about science which were summarized in the previous section reflected in students' portrayals of the nature of science? We now review the findings of our survey relating to students' views about the nature of science with this question in mind. Detailed accounts of the findings are given in Chapters 6, 7 and 9. Here we outline the main points relating to the three features of the nature of science of interest in this study, and draw attention to those which we see as being of particular educational relevance.

The purposes of scientific work

In general, students see science as addressing questions relating to physical and biological phenomena but not social phenomena. The relevance to society of a particular area of investigation was often given as a reason for scientists being engaged in it. Indeed, students tend to see the purpose of science as providing solutions to technical problems rather than providing more powerful explanations. Although younger students tend to define science in terms of their experiences of school science, older students draw on a wider range of experiences outside school in the ways they see scientific work.

There is a similar trend in the way students portray scientists, with students of primary age having limited and often stereotyped views. It is interesting to note that this stereotyping is not so apparent among secondary school students. In general, we found that older students tended to hold a benificent view of scientists as people whose work addresses important problems of relevance to society. The fact that students link the work of scientists to social issues is a matter that can be built on in schooling, by exploring the nature of scientific knowledge, its applicability and reliability, in the context of specific scientific work.

The nature and status of scientific knowledge

The ways that students see *the nature and status of scientific knowledge* are complex and involve their views of the nature of scientific enquiry, the nature of explanation and theories, and the way explanation and evidence are coordinated in the development and testing of knowledge claims.

Scientific enquiry

Students portray scientific enquiry in a number of ways. At the simplest level, students see scientific enquiry as a process of making observations about the world. A more elaborate view, and one commonly found at all ages, is that scientific enquiry involves making generalizations from observations. The most sophisticated view is that scientific enquiry involves the testing of models or theories. This latter view is not common even at age 16.

The status of theories and explanations

Sometimes, students see explanations as simply a redescription of an event or phenomenon. However, in most cases, they recognize that an explanation goes beyond what is given. The most common view is that explanation in science involves linking observable features in some way, either through establishing a causal link between a cause and an outcome, or by describing an empirically derived generalization. The view that scientific explanation can involve postulating theoretical entities and models is held by less than a quarter of 16-year-olds and by very few younger students. Even when students do consider explanation as involving a modelling process, most show no sign that they appreciate the conjectural nature of theories. Instead, models are seen to map on to events in the world in an unproblematic way, a perspective described by Carey *et al.* (1989) as a correspondence view of theories.

Coordination of explanation and evidence

The majority of students of all ages appreciate that theories are evaluated in terms of their consistency with evidence. From the questions that we asked in this study, it is not possible to comment on the more detailed criteria that students use to select between different theories or explanations (for further evidence on this aspect, see Samarapungavan 1992).

The extent to which students do evaluate theories appropriately using empirical evidence is, of course, a different type of question, and can only be assessed by observing their performance in context. Our results show a clear trend with age in students' levels of performance, with about a quarter of 9-year-olds and about three-quarters of 16-year-olds coordinating evidence and explanation consistently, and older students being more likely to evaluate theories correctly regardless of whether or not they believe the theory.

Science as a social enterprise

We found little evidence among the students in this study that they see science as a social enterprise. The dominant view is clearly that of the individual scientist undertaking his or her work in isolation. From the students' discussions of scientific disputes, there was evidence that some believed that scientific 'facts' would need to be 'put together' from a wide range of sources to reach 'the truth'. The process by which individual 'facts' might be checked or challenged within the scientific community, before becoming established, was not part of the students' picture of the way science is carried out.

Where conflicts arise in the scientific community, students consider differences of opinion between scientists as being due either to a lack of sufficient information (if they had more facts, then an answer would be clear), or to some form of bias (vested interest or personal pride). It is important to comment, however, that although students appear to have little, if any, knowledge of the social processes of the scientific community, they draw on a range of everyday social experiences to suggest how disputes might be resolved (for example, involving some form of adjudication or using the legal system as a model). Students clearly have resources to draw on, from their wider social experiences, to provide a starting point for understanding the particular social processes of science.

Finally, students have little awareness of the ways that society influences decisions about research agendas and priorities for particular science research programmes. Although students do see scientists investigating questions which are of concern to society as a whole, the mechanisms through which society influences decisions are rarely elaborated by students. The view which is most apparent is that scientists, through their personal altruism, choose to work on particular problems of concern to society.

| **Age-related trends in students' representations**

Many previous studies of students' views of the nature of science have compared students' responses (as described, for example, in the comprehensive review by Lederman 1992) with what are taken to be normative views of the nature of science. By contrast, in this study, our interest has not been to assess the extent to which students' views match some 'accepted' template, but rather to characterize the representations that students have of science and to document the profiles of these representations at different ages.

In order to characterize these broad trends we have proposed a general typology of students' epistemological reasoning. This typology, which is described in more detail in Chapter 8, identifies three qualitatively distinct epistemological representations, which we call *Phenomenon-based reasoning, Relation-based reasoning* and *Model-based reasoning*.

In *Phenomenon-based reasoning*, students make no distinction between observation and explanations; explanations are a redescription of events. Enquiry involves making observations of the world, either looking carefully at things or trying things to see what happens. In *Relation-based reasoning*, which is the most common form of reasoning used by secondary school students, students do distinguish between observation and explanation, but the explanation is seen as a generalization emerging from data, a general 'pattern' in the data. The purpose of scientific enquiry is to determine this pattern, in some cases through investigating possible associations between variables, or in others through producing an empirical generalization such as 'the thicker the wire, the lower the resistance'. *Model-based reasoning*, which was used by a minority of secondary school students by age 16, also distinguishes between observation and explanation. The explanation is now considered to be a model of the phenomena in question and elements in the model are seen to have a status (ontologically, and in terms of the extent of empirical support) which is different from that of the events which have to be explained. The model does not arise directly from the data but involves an act of imagination or conjecture. The predictions from the model can be checked against observations. However, although it is possible to refute a model as a result of contrary evidence, it is never possible to prove it is correct. To this extent, scientific models have a provisional status.

Overall, we see the youngest students as most likely to use *Phenomenon-based reasoning*. *Relation-based reasoning* is the most prevalent form of reasoning among younger secondary school students and, although it still predominates among 16-year-olds, a minority by this age show evidence of aspects of *Model-based reasoning*.

We recognize that this study cannot provide evidence for developmental patterns in the reasoning of individual students. We do argue, however, that the results are suggestive of a trajectory in the way students' views about the nature of science evolve and suggest that this information may be useful to consider when planning curriculum materials for different age groups of students.

As we argued in Chapter 9, however, it is important that these broad trends in reasoning at the population level are not misinterpreted. Each of these representations has a place in scientific reasoning and students will need to recognize which way of thinking is appropriate in particular situations. It is having these multiple perspectives available which is educationally important.

Portrayals of science in the curriculum

It is not possible from the results of this study to do more than speculate about reasons for students' different portrayals of science. The way scientific activity is represented in the media, especially television, and in the wider culture, may be influential. It could also be that there are psychological constraints on how students think about the nature and status of scientific knowledge. After all, we rarely operate in our daily lives in a way which considers knowledge about the world as anything other than clear and secure. Our daily activities of moving from place to place and manipulating objects in our environment are undertaken with a clear assumption of having secure knowledge about those objects and events. Considering knowledge to be provisional and conjectural may act to undermine deeply held preferences for certainty.

Research undertaken in the Piagetian tradition has, of course, already addressed this question of psychological constraints on learning. The hypothesis that has been advanced is that the logical capabilities of students are age-dependent and that some students will be unable to perform tasks which involve certain logical competencies because the capacity to do so has not yet been developed. The results of the **Theory and Evidence** probe in this study show that the majority of students were able to coordinate evidence and explanations appropriately when required. Fewer students recognized that a confirmatory result could not 'prove' an explanation right, whereas a contradictory one could 'prove' it was wrong. This aspect of our results may indicate that, even if there are such psychological constraints, these are not the limiting factor in the students' scientific representations.

There is evidence that the way science is portrayed in the school science curriculum has a major part to play in shaping students' views of science. The hypothesis that teachers' ideas and practices influence students' views on the nature of science has been the subject of a number of research studies. Zeidler and Lederman (1989), for example, have shown that when teachers use a language which distinguishes more precisely between the status of the different types of objects being referred to in lessons [for example, which differentiates scientific objects (atoms, ions) and objects in the world (chair, table)], then students tend to adopt a more sophisticated view of the nature of scientific knowledge.

In a series of recent studies, Roth and his colleagues have observed students planning and carrying out open-enquiry activities in science, and have explored the effect of these on students' perceptions of science (Roth and Bowen 1993, 1995). Roth uses changes in students' use of linguistic tools and in their discursive practices, as they discuss their work and seek to persuade others in the class of their conclusions, as indicators of their changing views of science and scientific enquiry. His work suggests that the design of laboratory tasks and the construction of the laboratory environment may have a significant influence on the images of scientific knowledge and enquiry which students develop.

Our experiences in science classrooms in the UK suggest that current teaching practices are portraying a limited perspective on the nature of science. The main emphasis in most lessons is on the intellectual products of science, not on the process of knowledge generation. The ideas of science are made to seem plausible through demonstration and their use is illustrated in a limited range of well-defined contexts. Rarely is the status of the knowledge questioned or even opened up for discussion.

A particularly obvious case of a restricted epistemological perspective being portrayed in science lessons can be seen in the National Curriculum for England and Wales (DES/WO 1991), where there is a requirement for students to undertake scientific investigations. The dominant view of scientific investigations, as enacted in classrooms, is, however, that of a multiple variable problem where students identify which independent variable affects a given dependent variable in a range of physical or biological contexts. This dominant view of scientific investigation thus reinforces *Relation-based reasoning* and fails to portray the much wider range of forms of empirical enquiry which scientists undertake. In particular, the view of scientific enquiry as involving the evaluation of a theory or model is rarely encountered. Furthermore, such investigations tend to be undertaken as individual enquiries, hence reinforcing the view that scientific knowledge is the product of individual endeavour.

Indeed, science is rarely portrayed in the curriculum as a social enterprise. Where the social relations of science are considered, these are most likely to be the external relations of science, for example, asking students to consider contested issues such as whether or not fluoride should be added to drinking water or where waste disposal sites should be sited. Furthermore, such tasks typically invite conclusions which depend more strongly on social and economic factors than on scientific ones, and encourage reasoning from commonsense knowledge rather than from formal disciplinary understandings. It is much less common for students to be asked to consider the internal relations of science and hence appreciate the steps that are taken from the work of a single scientist to the acceptance of a knowledge claim as part of the public knowledge of science. As we know, school science rarely considers fringe or contested science, and so there are few opportunities for students to be introduced to social processes through which knowledge claims are made.

| **What is worth teaching about the nature of science?**

Whether or not it is addressed explicitly, the ways that science lessons are conducted convey implicit messages about the nature of science. We are proposing here that explicit attention be given in the curriculum to this aspect of learning about science. We turn now to consider what might be included alongside the teaching of accepted scientific knowledge, in a science curriculum which also deals explicitly with the nature of science. The main focus of this part of the curriculum would be to emphasize 'science-in-the making' (Shapin 1992; Collins and Pinch 1993). Our proposal is for two aspects of the nature of science to be addressed explicitly: (1) the epistemological basis for making scientific knowledge claims and (2) science as a social enterprise.

Epistemological basis for scientific knowledge claims

Our aim in including this aspect is to increase students' awareness of the methods by which scientific knowledge claims are made and to promote an appreciation of both their power and limitations. We see three strands to this curriculum emphasis:

Evaluation of evidence

Knowledge claims in science are supported or refuted in the light of available evidence. Therefore, some appreciation of the nature of empirical data and systematic ways of collecting it and evaluating its quality or trustworthiness will be a necessary underpinning to an understanding of scientific knowledge claims.

The components that we see as important in gaining such an understanding are: an appreciation of the process of measurement and the inherent variability of measurements (necessary to understand the relationship between measurement and the notions of 'truth'); understanding concepts of accuracy, reliability, validity and replicability (important in evaluating the quality of data and therefore how much trust to put in it); ways of organizing the collection of data so that logical inferences can be made about the influence of specific variables or features of a system (this is what is traditionally seen as experimental design; however, rather than focusing on procedural aspects such as identification of dependent and independent variables, control of variables, etc., we see that emphasis needs to be placed on the *purpose* for which the data are being collected, i.e. whether valid inferences can be made which eliminate the possibility of other interpretations).

Nature of explanation

The purpose of science is to produce viable explanations for phenomena. This strand would make this explicit. It would illustrate how explanations go beyond observations, and that explanation involves an imaginative step or conjecture and, therefore, although explanations should be consistent with available evidence, they do not 'emerge' from the data. Different forms of explanation used in science, including empirical generalizations (such as Hooke's Law) and theoretical models (such as the wave theory of light), would be distinguished.

The evaluation of theories

Explanations or theories in science are evaluated in the light of evidence. To understand this, it is necessary to appreciate that theory is distinct from data. Evaluating a theory or comparing alternative theories requires making predictions from the theories and testing the consistency of these with available data. Any conflict between the predictions and the data may of course be due not only to a problem with the theory, but also with the accuracy of the data.

The core issue to be understood is the 'game-like' process that is involved. The rules of the game are that the only predictions that are allowed are those that follow from the theory. *Ad hoc* variations are not permitted. The task then becomes one of judgement as to whether or not the evidence is in keeping with the predictions from the theory. This involves more than a logical process of matching evidence and data; it involves an act of judgement about the quality of the data and the degree of match or mismatch which is obtained. This is, of course, a simplification of what happens in 'real science' where, for example, *ad hoc* adjustments have worked to long-term advantage. However, such an idealization provides a model which can be scrutinized in the light of more sophisticated situations at a later stage.

The generation and evaluation of predictions from theories

Making predictions about the behaviour of a natural phenomenon based on theoretical models is also problematic. To understand this, it is necessary to appreciate the abstract nature of theoretical knowledge, and the multiple reasons why predictions may not translate directly into observed behaviour in a given real-world context. In generating predictions in a given situation, it is necessary to consider the factors that need to be taken into account in modelling the phenomenon. Similarly, if predictions are not borne out by the empirical evidence, it is necessary to consider whether this is due to problems with the data collected, problems with the initial modelling of the phenomenon, or more fundamental problems with the theory.

We envisage that learning activities that address these strands would include practical investigations undertaken by students themselves. The purpose of the investigations, however, would be tuned to the specific strands identified above. There is also scope for using case studies from the history of science or from contemporary science, particularly in relation to the evaluation of theories.

Science as a social enterprise

We see three main strands which need to be addressed in relation to the social contexts of science.

How science as public knowledge comes about

This involves knowing about the ways in which public knowledge in science is developed through individual and communal effort. Scientific knowledge is not easily established. It is the result of a great deal of work, often by many people who are involved in trying to understand particular phenomena and communicate their ideas. Consensual scientific knowledge is arrived at by acting on the world, sharing the outcomes of this with others in the scientific community and having those outcomes publicly validated.

Scientific work is socially and politically embedded

This involves appreciating that scientific work always provides a partial story. Even with the best of intentions, scientific knowledge claims may be made from particular standpoints and result from particular programmes of research. In evaluating new and disputed knowledge, it is important, therefore, to ask in whose interests the knowledge is being developed.

Scientific knowledge-in-use

This strand requires students to appreciate that there are crucial differences between science in the laboratory and in the real-world. In the laboratory, situations are simplified so that an ideal system can be investigated and understood. Real-world situations, by contrast, are usually much more complex, with many more factors coming into play. As we indicated earlier, the extent to which a particular piece of scientific knowledge will apply in the complex real-world therefore involves acts of judgement, judgement about the assumptions on which the original knowledge is based and the extent to which these assumptions apply in the given situation. There is also uncertainty about what weighting to give different pieces of evidence in the situation of interest. Finally, in the decision-making process, forms of knowledge other than scientific knowledge, including economic, legal and ethical considerations, will often need to be brought to bear.

Helping students to understand how scientific knowledge is developed requires teaching material which focuses on the actual work of scientists and illustrates the internal social relations within science. To do this, case studies could be provided using written materials and videos which illustrate a range of scientific activities from routine laboratory work (e.g. a hospital lab histologist), to the 'normal' science undertaken in most industrial or university laboratories, to the revolutionary developments at the forefronts of particular fields of science. In addition to such case studies, it would be important for students to have contact with actual scientific work through visits and links between school science departments and industrial or university laboratories. Perhaps, however, the greatest insight into the way scientific knowledge is acquired will be gained by students if they themselves are engaged in real science activities. This will include not only their personal investigative work, but sharing their ideas and results at meetings and contributing to and reading journals. While it is recognized that such opportunities may only be available to a minority of students, there are interesting examples in the UK and elsewhere of successful programmes of scientific research in schools which indicate what might be possible in this respect (Albone 1993).

Learning activities which address the external relations of science, both the social and political aspects of scientific work, and the problematic features of applying scientific knowledge in practical situations, would need to be developed around carefully chosen contexts. We would see an important role for teaching materials which present students with situations about which there is controversy. Students would be expected to research the background information, deliberate the issues and come to an informed decision. Appreciation of the basic epistemological issues outlined earlier (reliability of data, possibilities of alternative explanations) will also need to be drawn on in such tasks. It would be important that the controversies are about issues which are seen by the students to be significant and relevant. There are many such issues which could provide a focus for materials of this sort, including controversies relating to the new genetics, the environment, transport policy, agricultural practices and health.

Types of learning activities and their sequencing

In developing a curriculum which would address these issues, attention would need to be given to the matter of progression in planning activities within the curriculum, so that students are introduced to the various aspects of the nature of the scientific enterprise in an appropriate sequence. Teaching examples and case studies would then need to be selected to illustrate appropriate aspects. Here we suggest an outline sequence, based on our survey, for the curriculum for 9- to 16-year-olds:

The epistemological strand

- systematic and careful data collection, and descriptive accounts of data sets (e.g. collecting and presenting information about pupils in the class);
- inductive generalizations (this could include examples from students'

own practical work, but also include case-study data from environmental surveys, epidemiology or public health);

- testing a theory or comparing competing theories (here the emphasis is on careful experimental design, relating the evidence to the theory and making a decision; examples can be taken from students' own work or case studies can be used).

The social contexts of science strand

Our study gives us less guidance in drawing up an appropriate sequence on this aspect. These suggestions are based as much on our experience of teaching in secondary schools as it is on the specific findings of this study:

- analysing the problems of applying scientific knowledge in specific practical situations; recognizing and analysing the science-based factors involved in the situation (e.g. safety features in motor cars);
- practical investigation within a group setting in which the aim is to establish or check a knowledge claim; including the communication of results to others and the analysis of different points of view (e.g. to establish the factors affecting a simple physical system, such as a bending beam or the period of oscillation of a vibrating object);
- evaluation of disputes about socioscientific issues; identification of issues and standpoints; decision-making (e.g. use of ionizing radiation in food preservation);
- major revolutions in science thinking, including the role of imagination in generating ideas, the reception of novel ideas by different social groups, the causes of disputes and their resolution (e.g. the Copernican revolution, Darwin's theory of evolution, the advent of quantum mechanics).

In this section, we have outlined what we would recommend being taught about 'the nature of science' and have made some suggestions about appropriate learning activities and their sequencing. We have based our recommendations on the assumption that there is a place for the explicit consideration of aspects of the nature of science to be included in the curriculum. This, of course, means that less time will be given to the teaching of what is conventionally referred to as the 'contents' of science. Obviously, very careful consideration will need to be given to what a reduced science content would include.

If the science curriculum includes some explicit discussion of the nature of science, then there is a strong possibility of conflict between this and the remainder of the science curriculum. Put at its starkest, it is likely that the teacher, when teaching well-established parts of accepted science, will adopt forms of language and will apply norms and use procedures in interpreting evidence and data (both first-hand data collected by pupil practical work or teacher demonstrations and second-hand data from textbooks) which are at odds with some of the things that might be said when teaching explicitly about the nature of science. As work on the nature of science is likely to form only a component of the whole science curriculum, there seems little doubt that the implied epistemology of the remainder (the teaching of 'normal science') will be what is communicated to students. This problem is explored by Millar (1989). Rich descriptions of learning episodes in science classrooms, such as those of Edwards and Mercer (1987) and French (1989), also reveal aspects of this tension. It is also implicit in critiques of discovery learning in science (Driver 1975; Atkinson and Delamont 1977; Wellington 1981; Harris and Taylor 1983), which highlight the conflicts which are inherent in lessons which purport to teach science concepts at the same time as providing insights into 'scientific method'. This is a tension which Duschl *et al.* (1992) suggest may exist inevitably between presenting a scientific theory in the context of 'justification' as an established piece of knowledge, and in the 'context of development' as an emergent knowledge claim. Russell (1983) has analysed teachers' classroom discourse, showing how their arguments and questions present a distorted picture of scientific reasoning and the role of evidence in relation to generalization and theory. The way science is presented in textbooks also conveys a picture of science which may be different from that which we would want to give when treating the nature of science explicitly (Kilbourn 1984; Sutton 1989).

We do not, therefore, underestimate the difficulty in helping students to understand the different purposes of the different sections of work in school science. However, it would be counterproductive to see the teaching on the nature of science being isolated completely from the teaching of science content. There will be important teaching opportunities to relate ideas from the basic introduction to epistemological issues to the teaching of specific content areas of science, thus supporting students' understanding of the nature of the knowledge with which they are engaging.

Using this wide range of activities in purposeful ways in the classroom depends crucially, of course, on competent and well-informed science teachers – a matter which is addressed in the next section.

| Teachers, teaching and the nature of science

Teachers' views on the nature of science and the relationship between teachers' conceptions of science and those of their students have been the subject of research for over a decade. Studies of secondary school science teachers' views of the nature of science indicate that they tend to be eclectic in their perspectives (Koulaidis and Ogborn 1989) and that they have not had opportunities themselves to reflect on and clarify their own views on the subject. Some extensive studies in classrooms have indicated that the dominant picture of science lessons is of teachers tending to represent science as a body of facts together with a set of mechanical empirical processes (Lakin and Wellington 1994). The extent to which this is a consequence of teachers' own views of the nature of science has been investigated, though the results are inconclusive (Lederman and Zeidler 1987; Duschl and Wright 1989; Brickhouse 1990).

In his comprehensive review, Lederman (1992: 351) argues that attention needs to be given to the complex situational variables involved in teaching:

> ... science educators' concerns must extend well beyond teachers' understanding of the nature of science, as the translation of these understandings into classroom practice is mediated by a complex set of situational variables. Although critically important, simply possessing valid conceptions of the nature of science does not necessarily result in the performance of those teaching approaches which are related to improving student conceptions.

We suspect that pressures of time and a curriculum represented in national policy documents or in textbooks as a body of established knowledge militates against teachers portraying the epistemological and sociological dimensions of science in an elaborated way. Students' expectations of science, as giving 'right answers', is also a factor which has to be borne in mind when attempting to introduce ideas about the nature and status of scientific knowledge. From the results of our study, we would expect secondary students to appreciate the social contexts of science: their discussions about scientific disputes indicated that they had a rich resource of knowledge about social processes in society on which to draw in addressing this aspect. Their lack of knowledge of the social processes of science is largely the result of a lack of any systematic attempt to make them aware of this dimension of scientific work. On the other hand, we suspect that students will find the epistemological strand more problematic to appreciate, since it challenges possibly deeply held views about reality and the nature of knowledge.

There have been innovative and dedicated science educators who over the years have explored effective ways of introducing school students to the nature of science (Aikenhead 1991; Solomon 1993), and some major curriculum projects have also attempted to take this aspect seriously (e.g. Rutherford *et al.* 1970). If more students are to be introduced to these ideas in schools, such practices will need to become more widespread.

There are multiple factors influencing the situation: the way teachers are trained; the availability of good teaching materials; the curriculum guidelines which teachers are required to follow and their associated assessment objectives; the ideas about science that graduate scientists who enter teaching have been socialized into during their education. All of these factors warrant attention if science is to be portrayed in schools in a more rounded and authentic way, in a way which recognizes its achievements and its limitations and most importantly in a way which shows it to be a human endeavour.

References

Aikenhead, G. (1987) High school graduates' beliefs about science–technology–society. 3: Characteristics and limitations of science knowledge. *Science Education*, 71 (4), 459–87.

Aikenhead, G. (1991) *Logical Reasoning in Science and Technology*. Toronto: John Wiley.

Aikenhead, G.S. and Fleming, R.G. (1975) *Science: A Way of Knowing*. Saskatoon: University of Saskatchewan, Department of Curriculum Studies.

Aikenhead, G., Fleming, R.W. and Ryan, A.G. (1987) High school graduates' beliefs about science–technology–society. 1: Methods and issues on monitoring student views. *Science Education*, 71 (2), 145–61.

Albone, E. (1993) Pupils as scientists. *Science and Public Affairs*, Summer, pp. 45–9.

American Association for the Advancement of Science (AAAS) (1967) *Science – A Process Approach*. Washington, DC: American Association for the Advancement of Science.

American Association for the Advancement of Science (AAAS) (1989) *Science for All Americans: A Project 2061 Report on Literacy Goals in Science, Mathematics and Technology*. Washington, DC: American Association for the Advancement of Science. (Also published subsequently by Oxford University Press, New York.)

Arnold, M. and Millar, R. (1993) *Students' Understanding of the Nature of Science: Annotated Bibliography*. Working Paper No. 11. Leeds/York: Centre for Studies in Science and Mathematics Education, The University of Leeds/Science Education Group, University of York.

Atkinson, P. and Delamont, S. (1977) Mock-ups and cock-ups: The stage management of guided discovery instruction. In P. Woods and M. Hammersley (eds), *School Experience: Explorations in the Sociology of Education*, pp. 87–108. London: Croom Helm.

Ayer, A.J. (1946) *Language, Truth and Logic*. London: Gollancz.

Ayer, A.J. (1981) *Hume*. Oxford: Oxford University Press.

Barnes, B. (1974) *Scientific Knowledge and Sociological Theory*. London: Routledge and Kegan Paul.

Barnes, B. and Dolby, R.G. (1970) The scientific ethos: A deviant viewpoint. *European Journal of Sociology, 2*, 3–25.

Barnes, B. and Shapin, S. (eds) (1979) *Natural Order: Historical Studies of Scientific Culture*. London: Sage.

Berger, P. and Luckmann, T. (1967) *The Social Construction of Reality*. Harmondsworth: Penguin.

Bernstein, R.J. (1976) *The Restructuring of Social and Political Theory*. London: Methuen.

Bhaskar, R. (1978) *A Realist Theory of Science*. London: Harvester Wheatsheaf.

Bloor, D. (1976) *Knowledge and Social Imagery*. London: Routledge and Kegan Paul.

Brewer, W. and Samarapungavan, A. (1991) Children's theories vs. scientific theories: Differences in reasoning or differences in knowledge. In R.R. Hoffman and D.S. Palermo (eds), *Cognition and the Symbolic Processes: Applied and Ecological Perspectives*, pp. 209–32. Hillsdale, NJ: Lawrence Erlbaum Associates.

Brickhouse, N.W. (1990) Teachers' beliefs about the nature of science and their relationship to classroom practice. *Journal of Teacher Education, 41* (3), 53–62.

Bronowski, J. (1964) *Science and Human Values*. Harmondsworth: Penguin.

Brown, S., Fauvel, J. and Finnegan, R. (1981) *Conceptions of Inquiry*. London: Methuen.

Bryce, T., McCall, J., MacGregor, J., Robertson, I. and Weston, R. (1983) *Techniques for the Assessment of Practical Skills in Foundation Science (TAPS 1)*. London: Heinemann.

Cameron, I. and Edge, D. (1979) *Scientific Images and Their Social Uses*. London: Butterworth.

Carey, S., Evans, R., Honda, M., Jay, E. and Ungar, C. (1989) 'An experiment is when you try it and see if it works': A study of grade 7 students' understanding of the construction of scientific knowledge. *International Journal of Science Education, 11* (5), 514–29.

Carnap, R. (1950) *Logical Foundations of Probability*. Chicago, IL: University of Chicago Press.

Carnap, R. (1966) *Philosophical Foundations of Physics: An Introduction to the Philosophy of Science*. New York: Basic Books.

Cartwright, N. (1983) *How the Laws of Physics Lie*. Oxford: Oxford University Press.

Chalmers, A.F. (1982) *What is This Thing Called Science?*, 2nd edn. Milton Keynes: Open University Press.

Chalmers, A.F. (1990) *Science and its Fabrication*. Milton Keynes: Open University Press.

Chambers, D.W. (1983) Stereotypic images of the scientist: The draw-a-scientist test. *Science Education, 67* (2), 255–65.

Cheek, D. (1992) *Thinking Constructively about Science, Technology and Society Education*. Albany, NY: State University of New York Press.

Chinn, C.A. and Brewer, W.F. (1993) The role of anomalous data in knowledge acquisition: A theoretical framework and implications for science instruction. *Review of Educational Research, 63* (1), 1–49.

Coles, M. and Gott, R. (1993) Teaching scientific investigation. *Education in Science, 154*, 8–11.

Collins, H.M. (1975) The seven sexes: A study in the sociology of a phenomenon, or the replication of experiments in physics, *Sociology, 9*, 205–24.

Collins, H.M. (ed.) (1981a) Knowledge and controversy: Studies of modern natural science. *Social Studies of Science* (spec. issue), *11* (1).

Collins, H.M. (1981b) Son of seven sexes: The social destruction of a physical phenomenon. *Social Studies of Science, 11* (1), 33–62.

Collins, H.M. and Cox, G. (1976) Recovering relativity: Did prophecy fail? *Social Studies of Science, 6*, 423–44.

Collins, H.M. and Pinch, T. (1993) *The Golem: What Everyone Should Know about Science*. Cambridge: Cambridge University Press.

Collins, H.M. and Shapin, S. (1986) Uncovering the nature of science. *Times Higher Educational Supplement,* 27 June, p. 13. Reprinted in J. Brown, A. Cooper, T. Horton, F. Toates and D. Zeldin (eds) (1986) *Science in Schools*, pp. 71–7. Milton Keynes: Open University Press.

Department for Education/Welsh Office (DFE/WO) (1995) *Science in the National Curriculum (1995)*. London: HMSO.

Department of Education and Science/Welsh Office (DES/WO) (1985) *Science 5–16: A Statement of Policy*. London: HMSO.

Department of Education and Science/Welsh Office (DES/WO) (1989) *Science in the National Curriculum*. London: HMSO.

Department of Education and Science/Welsh Office (DES/WO) (1991) *Science in the National Curriculum (1991)*. London: HMSO.

Driver, R. (1975) The name of the game. *School Science Review, 56* (197), 800–4.

Driver, R. and Oldham, V. (1986) A constructivist approach to curriculum development in science. *Studies in Science Education, 13*, 105–22.

Driver, R., Squires, A., Rushworth, P. and Wood-Robinson, V. (1994) *Making Sense of Secondary Science: Research into Children's Ideas*. London: Routledge.

Durant, J., Evans, G. and Thomas, G. (1989) The public understanding of science. *Nature, 340*, 11–14.

Duschl, R.A. (1990) *Restructuring Science Education: The Importance of Theories and their Development*. New York: Teachers College Press.

Duschl, R.A. and Wright, E. (1989) A case study of high school teachers' decision making models for planning and teaching science. *Journal of Research in Science Teaching, 26* (6), 467–501.

Duschl, R.A., Hamilton, R.J. and Grandy, R.E. (1992) Psychology and epistemology: Match or mismatch when applied to science education? In R.A. Duschl and R.J. Hamilton (eds), *Philosophy of Science, Cognitive Psychology, and Educational Theory and Practice*, pp. 19–47. Albany, NY: State University of New York Press.

Edwards, D. and Mercer, N. (1987). *Common Knowledge*. London: Methuen.

Feyerabend, P. (1970) Consolations for the specialist. In I. Lakatos and A. Musgrave (eds), *Criticism and the Growth of Knowledge*, pp. 197–230. Cambridge: Cambridge University Press.

Feyerabend, P. (1975) *Against Method*. London: Verso.

Finlay, F. (1983) Science processes. *Journal of Research in Science Teaching, 20* (1), 47–54.

Fleming, R.W. (1987) High school graduates' beliefs about science–technology–society. 2: The interaction among science, technology and society. *Science Education, 71* (3), 163–86.

Frankel, H. (1979) The career of continental drift theory: An application of Imre Lakatos' analysis of scientific growth to the rise of drift theory. *Studies in History and Philosophy of Science, 10*, 21–66.

French, J. (1989) Accomplishing scientific instruction. In R. Millar (ed.), *Doing Science: Images of Science in Science Education*, pp. 10–37. London: Falmer Press.

Freudenthal, G. (1986) *Atom and Individual in the Age of Newton*. Dordrecht: Riedel.

Funtowicz, S. and Ravetz, J. (1987) The arithmetic of scientific uncertainty. *Physics Bulletin, 38* (11), 412–14.

Giere, R.N. (1988) *Explaining Science: A Cognitive Approach.* Chicago, IL: University of Chicago Press.

Giere, R.N. (1991) *Understanding Scientific Reasoning,* 3rd edn. Fort Worth, TX: Holt, Rinehart and Winston.

Gilbert, G.N. and Mulkay, M. (1984) *Opening Pandora's Box: A Sociological Analysis of Scientists' Discourse.* Cambridge: Cambridge University Press.

Gillies, D. (1992) *Philosophy of Science in the Twentieth Century.* Oxford: Blackwell.

Gjertsen, D. (1989) *Science and Philosophy: Past and Present.* Harmondsworth: Penguin.

Gott, R. and Welford, G. (1987) The assessment of observation in science. *School Science Review, 69* (247), 217–27.

Gould, S.J. (1991) *Wonderful Life.* Harmondsworth: Penguin.

Gunstone, R. and Champagne, A. (1990) Promoting conceptual change in the laboratory. In E. Hegarty-Hazel (ed.), *The Student Laboratory and the Science Curriculum,* pp. 159–82. London: Routledge.

Hacking, I. (1983) *Representing and Intervening.* Cambridge: Cambridge University Press.

Hainsworth, M.D. (1956) The effect of previous knowledge on observation. *School Science Review, 37,* 234–42.

Hallam, A. (1975) Alfred Wegener and the hypothesis of continental drift. *Scientific American, 232,* 88–94.

Hann, K., Brosnan, T. and Ogborn, J. (1992) *Children and Teachers Talking Science (CHATTS) Project.* Working Papers 1–7. London: Institute of Education, University of London.

Hanson, N.R. (1958) *Patterns of Discovery.* Cambridge: Cambridge University Press.

Harré, R. (1972) *The Philosophies of Science.* Oxford: Oxford University Press.

Harré, R. (1986) *Varieties of Realism.* Oxford: Blackwell.

Harris, D. and Taylor, M. (1983) Discovery learning in school science: The myth and the reality. *Journal of Curriculum Studies, 15* (3), 277–89.

Hempel, C. (1965) The logic of explanation. In *Aspects of Scientific Explanation,* pp. 135–75. Baltimore, MD: Williams and Wilkins.

Hewson, M.G. (1986) The acquisition of scientific knowledge: Analysis and representation of student conceptions concerning density. *Science Education, 70* (2), 159–70.

Hodson, D. (1988) Towards a philosophically more valid science curriculum. *Science Education, 72* (1), 19–40.

Hodson, D. (1991) Assessing practical work: Why we shouldn't do it the Scottish way. *New Zealand Science Teacher, 66,* 10–15.

Husén, T., Tuijnman, A. and Halls, W.D. (eds) (1992) *Schooling in Modern European Society.* A Report of the Academia Europeae. London: Pergamon Press.

Inner London Education Authority (ILEA) (1988) *Science in Process.* London: Heinemann.

Johnson-Laird, P.N. (1983) *Mental Models.* Cambridge: Cambridge University Press.

Jones, B. (1974) Plate tectonics: A Kuhnian case? *New Scientist,* 29 August, pp. 536–8.

Karmiloff-Smith, A. and Inhelder, B. (1974) If you want to get ahead, get a theory. *Cognition, 3,* 195–212.

Kilbourn, B. (1984) World views and science teaching. In H. Munby, G. Orpwood and T. Russell (eds), *Seeing Curriculum in a New Light: Essays from Science Education,* pp. 34–43. Lanham, MD: University Press of America.

King, P.M., Kitchener, K.S., Davison, M.L. and Parker, C.A. (1983) The justification of beliefs in young adults: A longitudinal study. *Human Development, 26,* 106–116.

Kitchener, K.S. and King, P.M. (1981) Reflective judgement: Concepts of justification and their relationship to age and education. *Journal of Applied Developmental Psychology, 2,* 89–116.

Kitts, D.B. (1974) Continental drift and scientific revolution. *Bulletin of the American Association of Petroleum Geologists, 58,* 2490–96.

Klopfer, L.E. (1964) *History of Science Cases.* Chicago, IL: Science Research Associates.

Koulaidis, V. and Ogborn, J. (1989) Philosophy of science: An empirical study of teachers' views. *International Journal of Science Education, 11* (2), 173–84.

Kuhn, D., Amsel, E. and O'Loughlin, M. (1988) *The Development of Scientific Thinking Skills.* London: Academic Press.

Kuhn, T.S. (1962) *The Structure of Scientific Revolutions.* Chicago, IL: University of Chicago Press.

Kuhn, T.S. (1970) *The Structure of Scientific Revolutions,* 2nd edn, enlarged. Chicago, IL: University of Chicago Press.

Kuhn, T.S. (1977) *The Essential Tension.* Chicago, IL: University of Chicago Press.

Lakatos, I. (1970) Falsification and the methodology of scientific research programmes. In I. Lakatos and A. Musgrave (eds), *Criticism and the Growth of Knowledge,* pp. 91–196. Cambridge: Cambridge University Press.

Lakatos, I. (1978) *The Methodology of Scientific Research Programmes.* Cambridge: Cambridge University Press.

Lakin, S. and Wellington, J. (1994) Who will teach the 'nature of science'? Teachers' views of science and their implications for science education. *International Journal of Science Education, 16* (2), 175–90.

Larochelle, M. and Désautels, J. (1991) 'Of course, it's just obvious': Adolescents' ideas of scientific knowledge. *International Journal of Science Education, 13* (4), 373–89.

Latour, B. and Woolgar, S. (1979) *Laboratory Life: The Construction of Scientific Facts.* Princeton, NJ: Princeton University Press.

Laudan, L. (1977) *Progress and its Problems: Towards a Theory of Scientific Growth.* London: Routledge and Kegan Paul.

Layton, D., Jenkins, E., Macgill, S. and Davey, A. (1993) *Inarticulate Science? Perspectives on the Public Understanding of Science and Some Implications for Science Education.* Nafferton: Studies in Education Ltd.

LeGrand, H.E. (1988) *Drifting Continents and Shifting Theories.* Cambridge: Cambridge University Press.

Lederman, N. (1992) Students' and teachers' conceptions of the nature of science: A review of the research. *Journal of Research in Science Teaching, 29* (4), 331–59.

Lederman, N.G. and Zeidler, D.L. (1987) Science teachers' conceptions of the nature of science: Do they really influence teacher behaviour? *Science Education, 71* (5), 721–34.

Longino, H.E. (1990) *Science as Social Knowledge.* Princeton, NJ: Princeton University Press.

Losee, J. (1972) *A Historical Introduction to the Philosophy of Science.* Oxford: Oxford University Press.

Lynch, M. (1985) *Art and Artifact in Laboratory Science: A Study of Shop Work and Shop Talk in a Research Laboratory.* London: Routledge and Kegan Paul.

Mackenzie, D. (1978) Statistical theory and social interests: A case study. *Social Studies of Science, 8,* 35–83.

Masterman, M. (1970) The nature of a paradigm. In I. Lakatos and A. Musgrave (eds), *Criticism and the Growth of Knowledge*, pp. 59–90. Cambridge: Cambridge University Press.

Matthews, M. (1994) *Science Teaching: The Role of History and Philosophy of Science*. London: Routledge.

Maxwell, G. (1962) The ontological status of theoretical entities. *Minnesota Studies in the Philosophy of Science, 3*, 3–14.

Mead, M. and Metraux, R. (1957) The image of the scientist amongst high-school students. In B. Barber and W. Hirsch (eds), *The Sociology of Science*. New York: Free Press of Glencoe.

Merton, R. (1942) Science and technology in a democratic order. *Journal of Legal and Political Sociology, 1*. Reprinted as 'The institutional imperatives of science', in B. Barnes (ed.) (1972), *Sociology of Science*, pp. 65–79. Harmondsworth: Penguin.

Metz, K. (1991) Development of explanation: Incremental and fundamental change in children's physics knowledge. *Journal of Research in Science Teaching, 28* (9), 785–98.

Midgley, M. (1992) *Science as Salvation: A Modern Myth and Its Meaning*. London: Routledge.

Millar, R. (1987) Towards a role for experiment in the science teaching laboratory. *Studies in Science Education, 14*, 109–18.

Millar, R. (ed.) (1989) *Doing Science: Images of Science in Science Education*. London: Falmer Press.

Millar, R. and Driver, R. (1987) Beyond processes. *Studies in Science Education, 14*, 33–62.

Millar, R. and Wynne, B, (1988) Public understanding of science: From contents to processes. *International Journal of Science Education, 10* (4), 388–98.

Miller, J. (1983) Scientific literacy: A conceptual and empirical review. *Daedalus, 112* (2), 29–48.

Mulkay, M. (1979) *Science and the Sociology of Knowledge*. London: George Allen and Unwin.

Mulkay, M. (1985) *The Word and the World*. London: George Allen and Unwin.

Munby, H. (1982) *What is Scientific Thinking? A Discussion Paper*. Ottawa: Science Council of Canada.

National Curriculum Council (NCC) (1991) *Science: Non-statutory Guidance*. Section D. York: National Curriculum Council.

Newton-Smith, W.H. (1981) *The Rationality of Science*. London: Routledge and Kegan Paul.

Norris, S.P. (1992) Practical reasoning in the production of scientific knowledge. In R.A. Duschl and R.J. Hamilton (eds), *Philosophy of Science, Cognitive Psychology, and Educational Theory and Practice*, pp. 195–225. Albany, NY: State University of New York Press.

Office of Science and Technology (OST) (1993) *Realising Our Potential: A Strategy for Science, Engineering and Technology*. White Paper. London: HMSO.

Ogborn, J. (1992) *Explanation: A Theoretical Framework*. CHATTS Working Paper 4. London: University of London, Institute of Education.

Ogborn, J. (1994) *Science and Commonsense*. Unpublished manuscript. London: University of London, Institute of Education.

Open University (1981) *Course U202 Enquiry. Units 12–13: Scientific Revolutions*. Milton Keynes: Open University Press.

Pfundt, H. and Duit, R. (1994) *Bibliography: Students' Alternative Frameworks and Science Education*, 4th edn. Kiel: IPN.

Pickering, A. (1984) *Constructing Quarks*. Chicago, IL: University of Chicago Press.

Polanyi, M. (1958) *Personal Knowledge*. London: Routledge and Kegan Paul.

Popper, K.R. (1934) *Logik der Forschung*. Published in English (1959) as *The Logic of Scientific Discovery*. London: Hutchinson.

Putnam, H. (1962) What theories are not. In E. Nagel, P. Suppes and A. Tarski (eds), *Logic, Methodology and Philosophy of Science*, pp. 240–44. Stanford, CA: Stanford University Press.

Quine. W.V.O. (1951) Two dogmas of empiricism. Reprinted in *From a Logical Point of View*, 2nd edn, 1961. London: Harper Torchbooks.

Rapoport, A. (1957) Scientific approach to ethics. *Science, 125,* 796–9.

Roth, W.-M. and Bowen, G.M. (1993) An investigation of problem solving in the context of a Grade 8 open-enquiry program. *Journal for the Learning Sciences, 3,* 165–204.

Roth, W.-M. and Bowen, G.M. (1995) Knowing and interacting: A study of culture, practices, and resources in a Grade 8 open-enquiry science classroom guided by a cognitive apprenticeship metaphor. *Cognition and Instruction, 13,* 73–128.

Rowell, J.A. and Dawson, C.J. (1983) Laboratory counterexamples and the growth of understanding in science. *International Journal of Science Education, 5,* 203–15.

Royal Society (1985a) *The Public Understanding of Science*. London: The Royal Society.

Royal Society (1985b) *Science is for Everybody: Summary Report*. London: The Royal Society.

Russell, T.L. (1981) What history of science, how much, and why? *Science Education, 65* (1), 51–64.

Russell, T.L. (1983) Analysing arguments in science classroom discourse: Can teachers' questions distort scientific authority? *Journal of Research in Science Teaching, 20,* 27–45.

Rutherford, F.J., Holton, G. and Watson, F.G. (1970) *The Project Physics Course*. New York: Holt, Rinehart and Winston.

Ryan, A.G. (1987) High school graduates' beliefs about science–technology–society. 4: The characteristics of scientists. *Science Education, 71* (5), 489–510.

Samarapungavan, A. (1992) Children's judgements in theory choice tasks: Scientific rationality in childhood. *Cognition, 45* (1), 1–32.

Schauble, L., Klopfer, L.E. and Raghavan, K. (1991) Students' transition from an engineering model to a science model of experimentation. *Journal of Research in Science Teaching, 28* (9), 859–82.

Screen, P. (1986). The Warwick Process Science Project. *School Science Review, 68* (232), 12–16.

Shapere, D. (1982) The concept of observation in science and philosophy. *Philosophy of Science, 49,* 231–67.

Shapin, S. (1992) Why the public ought to understand science-in-the-making. *Public Understanding of Science, 1* (1), 27–30.

Shapiro, B. (1989) What children bring to light: Towards understanding what the primary school science learner is trying to do. In P. Fensham (ed.), *Development and Dilemmas in Science Education*, pp. 96–120. London: Falmer Press.

Shapiro, B. (1994) *What Children Bring to Light: A Constructivist Perspective on Children's Learning in Science*. New York: Teachers College Press.

Shen, B. (1975) Scientific literacy and the public understanding of science. In S.B. Day (ed.), *Communication of Scientific Information*, pp. 44–52. Basel: Karger.

Shipstone, D. (1985) Electricity in simple circuits. In R. Driver, E. Guesne and A. Tiberghien (eds), *Children's Ideas in Science*, pp. 31–51. Milton Keynes: Open University Press.

Siegel, H. (1988) Rationality and epistemic dependence. *Educational Philosophy and Theory, 20* (1), 1–6.

Smith, C., Carey, S. and Wiser, M. (1984) A case study of the development of size, weight and density. *Cognition, 21* (3), 177–237.

Solomon, J. (1989) The Nature of Science Series (*The Search for Simple Substances; Discovering the Cure for Scurvy; The Big Squeeze; Stars and Forces; Benjamin Franklin; Louis Pasteur*). Hatfield: Association for Science Education.

Solomon, J. (1991) Teaching about the nature of science in the British National Curriculum. *Science Education, 75* (1), 95–104.

Solomon, J. (1993) *Teaching Science, Technology and Society*. Milton Keynes: Open University Press.

Solomon, J. and Aikenhead, G. (eds) (1994) *STS Education: International Perspectives on Reform*. New York: Teachers College Press.

Solomon, J., Duveen, J. and Scott, L. (1994) Pupils' images of scientific epistemology. *International Journal of Science Education, 16* (3), 361–73.

Songer, N.B. and Linn, M.C. (1991) How do students' views of science influence knowledge integration? *Journal of Research in Science Teaching, 28* (9), 761–84.

Sutton, C. (1989) Writing and reading in science: The hidden messages. In R. Millar (ed.), *Doing Science: Images of Science in Science Education*, pp. 137–59. London: Falmer Press.

Tarling, D.H. and Tarling, M.P. (1971) *Continental Drift*. Harmondsworth: Penguin.

Thomas, G. and Durant, J. (1987) Why should we promote the public understanding of science? *Scientific Literacy Papers, 1*, 1–14. University of Oxford, Department of External Studies.

Trusted, J. (1987) *Inquiry and Understanding*. London: Macmillan.

van Fraassen, B.C. (1980) *The Scientific Image*. Oxford: Oxford University Press.

Wellington, J.J. (1981) 'What's supposed to happen, sir?' – some problems with discovery learning. *School Science Review, 63* (222), 167–73.

Wellington, J.J. (1989) *Skills and Processes in Science Education: A Critical Analysis*. London: Routledge.

Wynne, B. (1990) The blind and the blissful. *The Guardian*, 13 April, p. 28.

Zeidler, D.L. and Lederman, N.G. (1989) The effects of teachers' language on students' conceptions of the nature of science. *Journal of Research in Science Teaching, 26* (9), 771–83.

Ziman, J. (1967) *Public Knowledge*. Cambridge: Cambridge University Press.

Ziman, J. (1978) *Reliable Knowledge*. Cambridge: Cambridge University Press.

Appendix 1: Notes on the statistical test used

Calculation of χ^2 statistic to determine the statistical significance of age-related trends

The χ^2 statistic was used to evaluate the significance of apparent age-related trends:

$$\chi^2 = \sum \frac{(0 - E)^2}{E}$$

where O = the observed frequency and E = the expected frequency in the absence of any age-related trend.

Consider the following example. In Fig. 6.1, data are presented showing an apparent age-related increase in the number of students referring to empirical testing in justifying whether questions are scientific questions. The frequencies of responses referring to empirical testing are as summarized in the following contingency table:

	Empirical testing mentioned	Empirical testing not mentioned	Total
Age 9	38	177	215
Age 12	40	172	212
Age 16	76	197	273
Total	154	546	700

The null hypothesis, that there is no age-related trend in the number of students referring to empirical testing, was tested according to the following procedure.

Expected frequencies were calculated for particular responses at given ages according to the formula:

$$E = \frac{\text{Total coding decisions at a given age} \times \text{Total coding decisions for a given category}}{\text{Total coding decisions at all ages.}}$$

This results in the following table of expected frequencies:

	Expected frequency for empirical testing being mentioned	Expected frequency for empirical testing not being mentioned
Age 9	$215 \times 154/700 = 47.3$	$215 \times 546/700 = 167.7$
Age 12	$212 \times 154/700 = 46.64$	$212 \times 546/700 = 165.36$
Age 16	$273 \times 154/700 = 60.06$	$273 \times 546/700 = 212.94$

$(O - E)^2/E$ was calculated for each cell of the contingency table:

	$(O - E)^2/E$: empirical testing mentioned	$(O - E)^2/E$: empirical testing not mentioned
Age 9	$(38 - 47.3)^2/47.3 = 1.83$	$(177 - 167.7)^2/167.7 = 0.52$
Age 12	$(40 - 46.64)^2/46.64 = 0.95$	$(172 - 165.36)^2/165.36 = 0.27$
Age 16	$(76 - 60.06)^2/60.06 = 4.23$	$(197 - 212.94)^2/212.94 = 1.19$

χ^2 was calculated by totalling values for $(O - E)^2/E$, and a value of 8.98 was obtained. With two degrees of freedom, the trend was not significant at the 1% level ($p = 0.0112$).

Inspection of Fig. 6.1 shows that there was an apparent increase in the frequency of responses mentioning empirical testing after the age of 12. The null hypothesis that there was no increase in the frequency of responses mentioning empirical testing between the ages of 12 and 16 was tested using the following contingency table, in which data from students at ages 9 and 12 have been conflated:

	Empirical testing mentioned	Empirical testing not mentioned
Age 9 + Age 12	78	349
Age 16	76	197

Using a similar calculation, $\chi^2 = 8.89$, showing that the trend is significant between age 12 and age 16 at the 1% level ($p < 0.004$).

Appendix 2: Interview protocol for the probe Theory Stories

Rusting

Tom and Brian were at the seaside, as part of their school trip. They were walking along the promenade, leaning on the railings and watching the seagulls swooping down to the sea in search of fish. Brian noticed that the railings were similar to some back at school.

'These railings are just like the ones at school, next to the main gate.'

'Not quite the same! The ones at school are nowhere near as rusty as these ones', replied Tom.

Sure enough, the railings at school were painted white, and looked quite shiny and well kept. These railings were also painted white, but the brown rust was breaking out through the paint all over the place.

'I have a theory about that...', said Brian

What do you think Brian means by 'a theory'?
Have you any idea what his theory might be?

'Tell me then', said Tom, 'what do you think is going on?'

'Well', said Brian, 'it's to do with the sea. You know that the sea is salty?'

'Yes, go on . . .'

'Well, the saltiness of the sea is the answer!', said Brian.

'I can't see how that explains anything', said Tom. 'The salt's in the sea, and these railings are up here on the land. And anyway, how can salt make rust?'

'Well, you see', explained Brian, 'salt helps all sorts of things to go rusty. My Mum says that when they salt the roads it makes the underneath of the car go rusty. And it's easy to see how salt from the sea gets up to the rails. When there's storm the waves will splash water up here easily!'

'That's brilliant!', said Tom. 'That's it!'

| Or is it? Can the two boys really be sure that Brian's theory is correct? What could they do to check if Brian's theory really was correct?

| Balloons

Kay and Sarah were working in the science class with a tin container with a balloon stretched over the neck, so that the air is trapped inside the tin and the balloon. Their teacher, Miss Stark, asked them to heat the tin gently and watch what happens. When they do it, they notice that the balloon gets bigger.

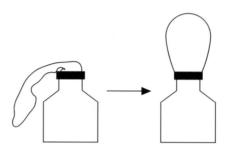

'The balloon's blowing up', said Kay. 'Why's it doing that?'
'It's the air', said Sarah. 'The air's going into the balloon.'
'How do you mean?', asked Kay.
'Well', said Sarah, 'when it gets hot, more air goes into the balloon. Look, you can see it's blowing the balloon up. There's more air in it now.'
'Yes', said Kay, but why does it do that?'
'Well, I have a theory about that', explained Sarah.

| What do you think Sarah means by 'a theory'? Have you any idea what her theory might be?

'Go on then', replied Kay, 'Tell me!'
'Well, I think it's because hot air rises. You know how you can feel hot air rising up from radiators and things. I think when we heat the tin the air inside gets hot and rises. So it goes into the balloon.'
Sarah then drew a picture to explain to Kay what she meant:

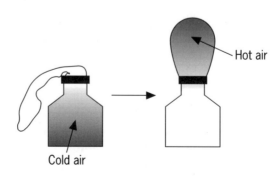

> Can the two girls be absolutely certain that Sarah's theory is right?
> What could they do to check if Sarah's theory really was correct?

Kay thought about Sarah's explanation for a minute. 'I'm not so sure', she said. 'What would happen if we held the tin upside down and then heated it? If the hot air rises, it will just go into the top half of the tin, won't it?'

'OK, let's try it', said Sarah. They let the tin cool down and then turned it upside down. When they heated it now, they found that the balloon got bigger . . . just as it had done before.

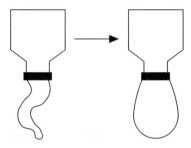

> Does this surprise you?
> What does this result tell the two girls?
> Does this prove that Sarah's theory was wrong?

'I didn't think that would work', said Sarah. 'I don't know what's happening to make it get bigger.'

They both thought for a minute. Then Kay said '*My* theory is that air expands when you heat it, so it needs more space, and that's why the balloon gets bigger.'

Sarah asked, 'What does "expand" mean?'

'It means get bigger and take up more space', explained Kay.

> The girls have now suggested two theories to explain why the balloon gets bigger when they heat the can:
>
> 1 Hot air rises
> 2 When you heat air it expands
>
> Do you think these theories are different?
> Which of these theories is best at explaining the things they have observed?
> Can they be absolutely certain that the better theory is right?
> What could they do to check if the better theory really is correct?

Germs

Adam and Alice had been left to look after themselves over the weekend. It was the middle of summer, and their parents had gone away for the weekend. They had decided that Adam and Alice were old enough to look after themselves for a couple of days, but their grandparents had been told to keep an eye on them.

Adam was in the habit of staying up late on Saturday night, and getting up very late on Sunday morning. This weekend was no exception. When he got downstairs to make some coffee, he found to his horror that there was no milk in the fridge.

'*Alice*! What have you done with the milk?'

'I might ask you the same thing. Did you have coffee last night after I went to bed?', she asked.

'Yes', answered Adam. 'But there was plenty left. What have you done with it?'

'Nothing! But *you* left it by the sink, under the kitchen window. And it is now completely off! I had to do without milk this morning too.'

This was her moment of triumph – she had wanted to get one over on her brother like this for days. He quickly changed the subject, however.

'I wonder why milk and other things go off quicker when they're not in the fridge?'

'I have a theory about that', answered Alice.

> What do you think Alice means by 'a theory'?
> Have you any idea what her theory might be?

'Go on', said Adam, pleased that he had changed the subject successfully. 'What is your theory?'

'Well, germs make things go off, don't they? And germs can grow better in the warm than in the cold!'

'I see', said Adam, 'That must be it!'

> But can they be absolutely certain that Alice's theory is right?
> What could they do to check if Alice's theory really was correct?

Appendix 3: List of working papers

All these Working Papers are available from The Business Secretary, CSSME, School of Education, University of Leeds.

Paper number	Authors	Paper title
Working Paper 1	Scott, P., Driver, R., Leach, J. and Millar, R.	Students' Understanding of the Nature of Science: Rationale and Methodology
Working Paper 2	Millar, R., Driver, R., Leach, J. and Scott, P.	Students' Understanding of the Nature of Science: Philosophical and Sociological Foundations for the Study
Working Paper 3	Driver, R., Leach, J., Millar, R. and Scott, P.	Students' Understanding of the Nature of Science: The Curricular Case for Teaching about the Nature of Science
Working Paper 4	Leach, J., Driver, R., Millar, R. and Scott, P.	Students' Understanding of the Nature of Science: Students' Characterisations of What Constitutes Scientific Questions
Working Paper 5	Leach, J., Driver, R., Millar, R. and Scott, P.	Students' Understanding of the Nature of Science: Students' Understanding of the Co-ordination of Theory and Evidence
Working Paper 6	Leach, J., Driver, R., Millar, R. and Scott, P.	Students' Understanding of the Nature of Science: Students' Characterisations of Experimental Enquiry

Paper number	Authors	Paper title
Working Paper 7	Leach, J., Driver, R., Millar, R. and Scott, P.	Students' Understanding of the Nature of Science: Students' Characterisations of the Nature of Theory
Working Paper 8	Leach, J., Driver, R., Millar, R. and Scott, P.	Students' Understanding of the Nature of Science: Students' Warrants for Belief in Scientific Knowledge Claims
Working Paper 9	Millar, R., Driver, R., Leach, J. and Scott, P.	Students' Understanding of the Nature of Science: Students' Awareness of Science as a Social Enterprise
Working Paper 10	Driver, R., Leach, J., Millar, R. and Scott, P.	Students' Understanding of the Nature of Science: Resumé and Summary of Findings
Working Paper 11	Arnold, M. and Millar, R.	Students' Understanding of the Nature of Science: Annotated Bibliography

Index